ISBN 978-0-265-90910-2
PIBN 10908191

This book is a reproduction of an important historical work. Forgotten Books uses
state-of-the-art technology to digitally reconstruct the work, preserving the original format
whilst repairing imperfections present in the aged copy. In rare cases, an imperfection in
the original, such as a blemish or missing page, may be replicated in our edition. We do,
however, repair the vast majority of imperfections successfully; any imperfections that
remain are intentionally left to preserve the state of such historical works.

THE SPRAGUE HOME
Nurses' Residence, 1750 West Congress Street

The Presbyterian Hospital Bulletin

CHICAGO, ILL.   JANUARY, 1930   NUMBER 70

*Published Quarterly by the Woman's Auxiliary Board. Officers of
the Woman's Board: Mrs. C. Frederick Childs, President;
Mrs. Clyde E. Shorey, Secretary; Mrs. Frederick
R. Baird, Corresponding Secretary; Mrs.
William Coffeen, Treasurer;
Editor of the Bulletin, Miss
Irma Fowler.*

Subscriptions, 50 Cents a Year, may be sent to Asa Bacon,
Superintendent, The Presbyterian Hospital of Chicago, or to
Mrs. William Coffeen, Hinsdale, Ill., or to
Miss Irma Fowler, 209 S. Oak Park Ave., Oak Park

EDITORIAL

With the small patient on the preceding page the Board sends its greetings for the New Year to all of its friends, associates and co-operators. The annual reports of our committees in this Bulletin are reports not only of the work of our Board members but of your support and interest.

3

ANNUAL MEETING

The 46th annual meeting of the Woman's Board was held Monday, January 6, at 11:00 o'clock, in the hospital chapel. Mr. Robert McDougal, president of the Board of Managers, presided.

The Rev. Dr. Ware gave the opening prayer.

Mr. McDougal voiced the appreciation of the Board of Managers for the help and inspiration from the Woman's Board and sketched the plans for the future of the hospital. His speech will be printed in full in the Bulletin.

The reports of the Recording and Corresponding Secretaries were read and accepted.

The Treasurer's report was read, accepted and placed on file.

Miss Brainerd, the head of the Occupational Therapy Department, presented some of the needs for even better results from the work of her department. Her ideal consists of the addition of a fountain and fireplace to the occupational shop, thereby creating a greater atmosphere of peace and relaxation, which is of definite therapeutic value to a patient.

Miss Lindom, the hospital librarian, gave a detailed report of her work since she began on September 1, 1929.

Dr. W. H. Boddy of the First Church gave an inspirational talk on "The Soul of the Hospital." This will be printed in the January Bulletin.

The report of the Nominating Committee was read by Mrs. L. T. Woodcock, chairman. The motion was made and carried to accept it and the Secretary was instructed to cast a white ballot for the following:

HONORARY PRESIDENT
Mrs. David W. Graham

PRESIDENT
Mrs. C. Frederick Childs

VICE PRESIDENTS
Miss Helen Drake	Mrs. Wilton B. Martin
Mrs. Frederick T. Haskell	Mrs. Ernest E. Irons

RECORDING SECRETARY
Mrs. Clyde E. Shorey

ASSISTANT RECORDING SECRETARY
Mrs. Earle B. Fowler

CORRESPONDING SECRETARY
Mrs. Frederick R. Baird

TREASURER	ASSISTANT TREASURER
Mrs. William Coffeen	Mrs. E. L. Beatie

4

Advisory Council

Mrs. Frederick W. Crosby
Mrs. Ernest A. Hamill
Mrs. David W. Graham
Mrs. Perkins B. Bass
Mrs. Charles L. Bartlett
Mrs. Henry M. Curtis
Mrs. Albert B. Dick
Mrs. Henry C. Hackney
Miss Jessica Jenks

Mrs. John B. Lord
Mrs. J. P. Mentzer
Mrs. L. Hamilton McCormick
Mrs. George R. Nichols
Mrs. C. K. Pomeroy
Mrs. John Timothy Stone
Mrs. Wm. R. Tucker
Mrs. Ezra J. Warner
Mrs. J. C. Welling

Executive Committee

Term Expiring December 31, 1932

Mrs. Howard Henderson
Mrs. Asa Bacon
Mrs. O. H. Jones
Mrs. S. W. Findley
Mrs. Agnes White

Mrs. Lawrence Dunlap Smith
Mrs. C. J. Rittenhouse
Mrs. Alfred L. Wilson
Mrs. Carey Culbertson

To Fill Unexpired Terms

Mrs. W. E. Sharp   Mrs. Raymond A. Smith

Member of Nominating Committee

Mrs. Frank L. Smith

Mrs. Childs then took the chair and expressed the thanks of the Board to Mr. McDougal and Dr. Boddy. She then called for a rising vote of thanks to Miss McWilliams, for her services as treasurer.

Miss McMillan expressed the thanks of the School of Nursing for the Christmas present of new equipment to the school. She had on display the models of the ear and eye.

The By-law defining the personnel and duties of the Appropriations Committee was read by the Secretary.

The meeting was adjourned.

Respectfully submitted,

Elizabeth D. Shorey.

REMARKS BY ROBERT McDOUGAL, PRESIDENT OF THE BOARD OF MANAGERS

The United States Government is rightly called the greatest business in the world. The Presbyterian Hospital is a business enterprise vast and far reaching. The Woman's Board of the hospital is by itself an impressive business with receipts the last fiscal year of $35,000, expenditures $23,000, and a balance on hand of $12,000.

From this sound business base come forth through superior qualities of head and heart ministrations to the sick and unfortunate beautiful and worthy. It may fairly be said, however, that the best work of the Woman's Society is not here, but in its unseen though powerful influence exerted by character, conduct and example to inspire in others recognition and a part in hospital work which clearly belongs to the great plan of the Almighty whose dominion is an everlasting dominion, whose kingdom is from generation to generation, and the heart of which is to serve and to minister unto others.

The foundation is permanent and true because it has in it the element of the Divine. Your work in assisting to relieve and comfort and restore to health, is a revelation and an inspiration, because health is the foundation on which reposes the happiness of the people and the power of the country and, without it, neither science, nor art, nor strength, nor wealth, nor eloquence, can have anything to show.

A word about future needs and opportunities.

Just as you greatly serve the hospital so the hospital greatly serves the public. It is now in need of five to ten millions of money to revamp and expand plant and equipment to keep abreast of the forward march of the city in years to come. It has been said there are upwards of one hundred Presbyterian or kindred churches in the metropolitan district of Chicago. Whether the number of such churches is in fact larger or smaller than this estimate, would it be out of place to ask that the Woman's Board take steps to present to them their raising a half million dollars as a participatory share in this project. This is a tentative suggestion which you would not be expected to take action upon until the plan in its entirety has been launched by the Board of Managers.

Those charged with the management of the hospital's business, as well as the hospital's friends everywhere, will be hard put to successfully meet the situation.

Needing such aid at your hands I submit whether, when the time comes, reasonable financial aid should not be given.

The Board of Managers of the Presbyterian Hospital expresses to its distinguished Auxiliary, the Woman's Board, gratitude for the past and high hopes for the future. It earnestly commends you for the excellence of able and unselfish achievement—and through you also extends to the pastors and to the many churches over which those pastors preside and which you represent, full appreciation of intelligent cooperation and energetic support throughout the year.

The Board of Managers tenders you its admiration as well as its gratitude. You are doing God's work. The Almighty has his own purposes which poor man cannot always fathom but whatever the Plan is, or may be, I doubt not through the ages one increasing purpose runs.

I thank you for the opportunity and privilege of giving this greeting and opening this meeting.

THE SOUL OF THE HOSPITAL

Rev. William A. Boddy

Mr. McDougal, Ladies of the Auxiliary Board and of the Hospital Staff:

It is a pleasure to be here today if only to add my word of appreciation to the intelligent and sustained interest of the consecrated womanhood of this Board in the welfare of the Presbyterian Hospital and those to whom it ministers. I could spend the few minutes which are mine in speaking only in praise of your work without giving myself to exaggeration or deceit. Your works praise you in the gate or, to drop the figure, they applaud you in all the wards and rooms of this institution devoted to human helpfulness. On the other hand, I might give my time to congratulating ourselves together on the efficiency, the humanness and the general serviceableness of this great hospital in which we are interested. I could do that without departing from the truth because we have here a hospital which, in the skill of its medical and nursing staff and the high tradition of its ministry, cannot be excelled in the country. But I am here on more rewarding business than to minister to our self-complacency and to that I address myself.

I would like to pause, however, to say a word of sincere appreciation for the lovable personality, the enlightened enthusiasm and the inspiring leadership of Mr. McDougal who has presided over our Board of Managers for the last sixteen months. He has made a permanent contribution to the Presbyterian Hospital and he has enriched the lives of all of us who, through this association, have enjoyed his friendship.

The first duty of a follower of Christ in the presence of any misfortune is to seek the quickest means of giving relief. There is no following of the Gentle Seer of Galilee apart from a new enthusiasm for humanity. He said: "I am come to seek and to save that which is lost." And surely that means He came to redeem from every influence whatsoever which would dwarf and impoverish personality. He said: "I am come that ye might have life and that ye might have it more abundantly." Whatever else that means, surely it suggests that Jesus is on the side of all that makes for the joy of health and the verve of life and that He is against all that makes for the limitations and thwartings of disease.

And so it is very natural that the first hospitals should have been established by people who were followers of Jesus and that ever since His disciples have been in the business of ministering to the fuller health of the people. The Christian hospital is a tool or agency of healing provided by the Church and put into the hands of men trained scientifically in the diagnosis and healing of sickness. It is an instance, or should be, where science and religion meet in the glory of human service. A hospital such as this would be almost entirely unavailable were it not for great religious and philanthropic foundations. I believe it can be successfully maintained that, except in the case of very small private institutions and one or two larger ones, the most successful hospitals are not conducted by private enterprise for profit. Certainly a Christian hospital would never capitalize the misfortunes of the sick and any profits which accrued, if profits ever do accrue from hospitals, would be put back into larger charitable service.

But I have asked myself what makes a hospital distinctly Christian? Charitable service, certainly that is one thing—but that can be obtained elsewhere; kindly service which puts the welfare of the patient above all other consideration is certainly a Christian point of view—but I do not think that is wholly confined to Church hospitals. For instance, I visited in a hospital conducted by a great business corporation for the good of its employees. It is efficient, it has a scientific staff, it is not operated for profit; the patient is the chief concern of everyone from the management to the maids. *But,* you know I am old-fashioned enough to believe that I ought to find something in the Presbyterian Hospital, operated on a great Christian foundation, that I cannot expect to find in that other hospital.

And I think that difference ought to be found in that indefinable thing we call atmosphere or in the soul of the institution. It is one thing to give a cup of cold water; it is another thing to give it *in Christ's Name.* Why is it? After all, is not water just as good for the quenching of the thirst whether it be given in careless unconcern or with the blessing of Christ? No, it is not. A man's physical needs are all bound up with spiritual longings and he who gives a cup of water in Christ's Name relieves a bodily want and, at the same time, enlarges a spiritual horizon; a cup of water given in Christ's Name has linked a man's need to a universal *love* and a cosmic benevolence in which alone can be found that which satisfies the hungry heart of humanity. When you give a cup of water—in Christ's Name—that means with Christ's motive, in Christ's spirit of self-forgetting love, you reach the infinite through the finite.

I had a good illustration of that the other day. A man came to me for counsel. He was a well-dressed, highly educated man. He said: "I want you to pray with me. For the first time in my years I find life is too difficult for me." By questioning, I found he had been robbed and he was a stranger in the city and had forty cents in his

9

pocket. He would not take any help but he would work. Well, of course, I hear many such stories. But I took this man to lunch with me and then gave him work helping sweep floors—he was a geological engineer who had done important work over the world. After about three days, he came to me and said: "Mr. Boddy, I'm all right. I've got hold of myself. I remember now that I have got friends though I've been out of the country for many years. But somehow I've felt whipped; I had even forgotten how to go about getting in touch with people who would value my service." The result was this—that man sent a message to New York and a wire came back from a great oil company to their local representative to tie him up to a contract immediately. He begins with at least $18,000 a year. But he came back and said to me: "It was not the money I got at the Church which saved me—it was something that reintegrated my inner life." It was not the few dollars—it was Christ's Name that did it. Through a finite want, an infinite need had been reached.

Now I think that without blare of trumpets but without apology, we should extend the service of this Hospital in Christ's Name and for His sake. I am the last person who would tolerate any revivalistic effort in a hospital or any intrusion upon the privacy of a man's soul but, after all, when one enters a Christian institution, he ought to expect to find there something distinctly Christian.

In one hospital of which I have heard, every patient upon entering receives, perhaps with his first tray, a beautifully wrought message telling him that his sickness is of vital concern not only to those who minister to him within the walls of the hospital, but to others who help to maintain it in the name of religion, and that, during his stay as a patient, he and all who are dear to him will be commended by unknown friends to the God and Father of us all. Then, too, I confess I should like to see some carefully chosen religious painting or poem upon the wall of every sick room. Again and again, I have visited patients in Catholic and Episcopal hospitals who have told me of their satisfaction in overhearing the brief, quiet service conducted on each floor each morning for the nurses and perhaps for others who could attend. I know we have a weekly service here and a fine chaplain and yet I dare to wonder if something else could not be done to indicate we give our service because of Christ. I find in a Christian home an atmosphere, something of quietness and assurance, the hint of an unseen comrade which I do not find in the best non-Christian home. That is what I covet for this hospital in ever-increasing depth. The Church, in my judgment, makes a mistake when it modifies its great foundations, in the interests of greater wealth, merely to a humanistic service, however help-

10

ful. Man is a blend of body and spirit and the glory of a Christian hospital ought to be that it ministers to both at the same time. I am not thinking of preaching or evangelizing but of the impregnating of an institution with such a spirit that every nurse, interne, physician and patient who enters it shall feel that he is upon consecrated ground.

Of course the commonplace things which I have suggested as possibly helpful are, after all, quite secondary. The atmosphere of an institution is created by the quality of the men's souls who live and work within it. It is the silent, unseen outgoing of the Christian spirit which does most to make an institution distinctly Christian. I am sure we have that here in a surprising degree. No one could be a patient here as I have been in the past few weeks and not feel the impress of the dedicated personalities who are investing their lives in this service.

Then, too, we are learning more and more of what an atmosphere of hopefulness and faith may contribute to the healing of the sick. When we have thrown aside all the vagaries of professional faith healers, there remains an enormous psychological contribution which a vital religious attitude has to make toward the cure of sickness. All that makes for courage and confidence and the integration of the personality lifts a weight off the nerve cells and gives nature and science a better chance to perform their curative functions. Dr. Oliver, a noted psychiatrist who just has taken a Pulitzer prize for the notable book of the year, has been writing upon the immeasurable hindrance of many psychic attitudes which interfere with the work of the physician. He says this: "You who walk all day among small, irritating fears that beset every inch of your dark path—fears of your own incompetency, of your inefficiency, of your failing powers of application and success, fears about your body and its functions, fears of infection of serious illness, of helpless, hopeless old age, and you who seek to hold off these fears a little by all sorts of mental makeshifts—there is only one sure help—one sure release from your servitude. And it lies near at hand. Sit you down, in quiet, by the river of God's presence. And, as a boy tosses stones into a pond, so cast your fears one by one into the waters of God's love. They shall disappear. You shall never see them again. You shall walk on, a free man once more. Only—only—in the future, do not wander too far from the river bank."

I would see that river of God's presence flowing, more and more, deeply and serenely through this institution dedicated in Christ's Name to healing the hurts of humanity.

11

COMMITTEE REPORTS

The total receipts from committees for the year 1929 are as follows:

Associate Membership................$1,384.00
Chicago Children's Benefit League...... 2,655.21
Child's Free Bed.................... 1,909.00
Contributors' Fund.................. 5,978.00
Permanent Linen Fund.............. 3,266.00
Pledge Fund........................ 3,992.00

DELICACIES COMMITTEE

The report of the Delicacies Committee for 1929 is as follows:

4126 glasses of jelly.
  76 bottles of grape-juice.
  51 cans of vegetables.
  40 pints of marmalade.
  91 cans of fruit.
   2 pounds of tea.
   2 quarts of honey.
   1 pound of butter.
  ½ gallon of peaches.

Thirty churches and four doctors' wives contributed this amount.

Mary A. Mentzer,
May N. Olmsted,
Chairmen.

FURNISHING COMMITTEE

The Furnishing Committee has made the reception room in the Jones building attractive with window hangings in a red toile patterned chintz and expect to do more to this room as opportunity offers. The reception room of the Pavilion has had certain additions to the furnishings; a new striped material in bronze and blues makes cheerful slip-covers in place of the plain light colored linen, and for contrast a glazed, small flowered black chintz covers the straight chairs. New lamps add their bit of glowing color to the room. All of these fittings bring out the charm of the hangings purchased two years ago.

The Committee also decided to make a beginning on the private maternity floor where one room, already remodeled by the hospital, was furnished in a different style from the other hospital rooms.

The alcove at the south end of this floor has been beautifully furnished. At the windows are stunningly patterned shades instead of the plain white curtains. There is a lovely lamp on the desk and a new settee and chairs and little table. These and the new rug, a soft plain green, all add their quota of comfort for anyone waiting there. You will see that the Committee, by concentrating on these waiting-rooms, are impressed with the realization that they also suffer who only sit and wait.

We expect to make the internes' rooms more homelike and would like to do more in the Jones reception room soon. Our appropriation was one thousand dollars and it is through the kindness of one of our committee members, Miss Elizabeth Browning, that our money has covered so many beautiful furnishings.

Mrs. Thomas Kelly, whose death was an especial loss to this Committee as well as to the Board, was greatly in favor of furnishing the alcoves of each floor where the families of patients on that floor spend so many anxious hours.

The collection of soap wrappers from Kirk and Company has provided the hospital with many dozen teaspoons and there was added the always generous gift from the company.

Mary M. Bass, Chairman.

OCCUPATIONAL THERAPY DEPARTMENT

The occupational therapy department has pursued the even tenor of its way through the eleventh year of its existence. The present staff consists of a director and two assistants. In addition to therapeutic work with the patients, every student nurse in the institution receives three weeks of instruction in the department. Equipment for etching by means of celluloid plates was added to the other resources of the shop during the past year, and this has appealed to many patients. An aquarium stocked with tropical fish was purchased last fall, and this has stimulated the interest of quite a group of patients. Several patients have taken snails from the aquarium when they went home from the hospital. The department has had a larger number of visitors than usual during the past year and in some cases advice has been sought about installing new departments or reorganizing departments already established. Since last June, two members of the staff have left to further pursue the study of Occupational Therapy, one at the St. Louis School of Occupational Therapy and one at the University of Iowa.

ANNUAL MEETING OF BOARD OF MANAGERS OF PRESBYTERIAN HOSPITAL

The annual meeting of the Board of Managers of the Presbyterian Hospital was held on January 22d. Mr. Robert MacDougal gave his final report as president, expressing his appreciation of the support given him by the Board of Managers, the staff, and superintendents of the hospital and School of Nursing and the Woman's Board. He announced that Mr. Alfred T. Carton has accepted the office of president, which is cause for congratulation by all the Board.

The report of the treasurer, Mr. Solomon Smith, disclosed that more than $167,000 had been spent for charity work in 1929.

Mr. Bacon, as superintendent of the hospital, reported that since its foundation in 1883, the hospital has cared for 245,000 people. In that time the average stay has been reduced from 28 days to 12 days; the rate of mortality from 6+% to 3—%. In 1929, 11,800 people were cared for. Of that number, 4,000 paid in full, 5,900 paid part of their cost and 1,800 paid nothing for their treatment.

The Reverend Mr. Ware gave the report of his services as chaplain in the hospital throughout the year.

Miss Helena McMillan, principal of the School of Nursing, reported that there has been an average of 280 nurses resident in the home. Of that number 179 are on duty in the hospital, 61 are graduates and 118 students. Of the remaining number there are those on duty in the medical and surgical clinics of Rush Medical College, also the Out-Maternity Department and pre-natal clinics of that college. In this department alone, 3,240 calls were made last year. Others man the Central Free Dispensary where 370 patients are cared for each day. Still others are procuring training in contagious and mental work at Durand Hospital and the Chicago Psychopathic. The high standard of service maintained by the hospital which shortens the length of stay of the patient, demands greater efficiency in nursing, which in turn necessitates the employing of more graduate nurses. The Endowment Fund has reached $29,000. Any increase in this amount will help in giving more income for greater knowledge by the graduate nurses and the opportunity to place more graduates in the hospital.

A motion expressing the appreciation of the Board for the work of Miss McMillan was passed.

Dr. John Timothy Stone voiced the sentiments of the ministers of the city in pledging their cooperation in the work of the hospital.

The report of the nominating committee was read by Mr. Douglass, presenting as managers to succeed themselves, Mr. Horace W. Armstrong, Mr. John D. Drake, Mr. R. Douglas Stuart, Mr. James Hall Taylor and Mr. Thomas E. Wilson.

The meeting then adjourned and the Board reconvened to elect its officers for the ensuing year.

In the year 1904, Dr. Fletcher Ingalls performed the remarkable feat of removing a fragment of pipe stem from the bronchus of a patient with the aid of the Fluoroscope at the Presbyterian Hospital, at Chicago. This remarkable operation caused a great deal of interest and marked the beginning of an era of work that has since saved the lives of many. Since this successful pioneering, this class of work has been carried on steadily, but many handicaps have presented themselves which, in a way, retarded its progress, such as inflexible and unwieldy apparatus.

A radical departure in equipment has been placed on the market, which new apparatus greatly enhances the value not only of this work, but that of removing foreign objects from other parts of the body, successfully setting of fractures under the Fluoroscope, etc. This new apparatus is so constructed that it can be handled with perfect ease and safety, the X-ray tube being completely housed in oil and can be moved about the patient so that any desired angle can be obtained without the necessity of moving the patient.

The board of managers of the Presbyterian Hospital of Chicago, keeping pace with progress and being quick to recognize the vast importance of doing this class of work with the utmost ease and safety, and also recognizing that in this new unit they have found their ideal, are making a Christmas present to the hospital of. this unit completely installed in a separate room adjoining the present X-ray Department.

The photograph shows some foreign objects extracted from the bronchus at the hospital the past year.

NOT A CROSS WORD PUZZLE, BUT OBJECTS TAKEN FROM OESOPHAGUS, BRONCHUS AND THE LUNGS

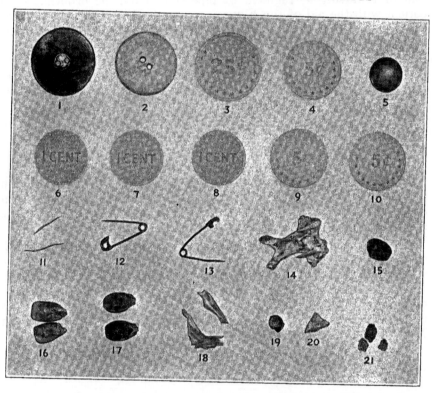

1 and 2, Buttons; 3, 4, 6, 7, 8, 9 and 10, Coins; 5, Bead; 11, Pieces of wire; 12 and 13, Safety pins; 14, Oyster shell; 15, Cherry pit; 16, Corn; 17, Melon seeds; 18, Pieces of bone; 19, Shell; 20, Piece of eraser; 21, Peanuts.

FREE BEDS AND MEMBERS

A donation of $50,000 entitles the donor to name a twelve-bed ward, which shall remain as a perpetual memorial to the donor, or any other individual he wishes.

A donation of $20,000 carries the same privileges for a four or six bed ward.

A donation of $10,000 entitles the donor to designate a room in the Private Pavilion which shall be named as desired by the donor and remain as a perpetual memorial.

A donation of $7,500 designates a bed in perpetuity.

A donation of $5,000 designates a bed during one life.

A donation of $5,000 designates a bed in the Children's Ward in perpetuity.

A donation of $300 annually designates a free bed in the general wards.

A donation of $100 or more constitutes the donor a life member of the institution.

A yearly donation of $10 constitutes an annual member.

FORM OF BEQUEST

I give and bequeath to the Presbyterian Hospital of the City of Chicago, incorporated under the law of the State of Illinois, the sum of .... Dollars, to be applied to the use and benefit of the said hospital, under the direction of the managers thereof.

FORM OF DEVISE

I give and devise to the Presbyterian Hospital of the City of Chicago, incorporated under the law of the State of Illinois, all that, etc. [*describe the property*], to be had and holden to the said the Presbyterian Hospital of the City of Chicago, and their successors and assigns, for the use and benefit of the said hospital.

ALUMNÆ NOTES

Officers elected at the annual meeting held January 6th are:

President............:....................Florence Cooper, class of 1927
1st Vice-President.................Evelyn Munson, class of 1924
2nd Vice-President....................Ella Farwell, class of 1919
Recording Secretary..............Elizabeth Lehman, class of 1925
Treasurer....................Mrs. Dick Van Gorp, class of 1924
Corresponding Secretary.............Alice Spellman, class of 1928
Ass't Corresponding Secretary........Ella Van Horn, class of 1921

Board of Directors............{ Amelia Mazzorana, class of 1924
Edith Stehle, class of 1921
Mary Cutler, class of 1916

Miss Cutler, chairman of the Bazaar Committee, reports that the returns for this year's combined sales total $1,401.97.

Several of the graduate nurse staff are attending a course in hospital administration being given during the winter months by Dr. Malcolm T. MacEachern, Director of Hospital Activities of the American College of Surgeons, while quite a number of the head nurses have signed up for a course on supervision by Miss Gladys Sellew, who is the author of a text book on that subject and an experienced supervisor. Both of these courses have been made possible through the yearly Educational Fund appropriated for such purposes by the Woman's Board of the Hospital, as is also a course of six lectures now being given at the Sprague Home by Mrs. Theodosia Crosse on Correct Social Usage.

The instructors of the school are rejoicing over further evidence of the generosity of the Woman's Board in a Christmas gift of money sufficient in amount to meet fully the needs of the class room equipment. With this gift there have already been purchased a new skeleton, enclosed in a case; a manikin; a disarticulated skull and models of the eye and the ear. The gift will also provide slides for an anatomy, possibly some desired charts, and other long-needed equipment.

Mrs. George S. Nicolls made an individual gift of 24 volumes of the Library Copy of the Encyclopedia Britannica on a stand of its own. All of these are much treasured and make an important addition to the teaching ability of the school.

Prizes are being offered for any authentic information regarding nursing of the past in Illinois. The Illinois State Nurses' Association is compiling the History of Nursing in this State and is seeking assistance. Mrs. Van Frank, Director of Nursing Headquarters, will supply details.

1908

P. K. Jones paid a short visit to us between Christmas and New Year's on her way from New York to California. Miss Jones plans to be in Paris in the early summer and will be associated with the American Hospital.

1912

Catherine Buckley, Dean of the School of Nursing, University of Cincinnati, in Chicago for a few days in January, was among our graduates who visited us.

1914

Edna M. Burgess, on furlough from Persia after seven years of service, was present at the Alumnæ meeting, January 7th, and gave a short talk on her experiences.

1915

Mrs. Ernest Williams (Edith C. Boone) is spending the winter in California.

Hilda G. Stickley, during a Christmas vacation, called to see us and tell of her new work, which is in connection with the Detroit Visiting Nurse Association. Since the completion of a course in muscle corrective work in Boston, she has been specializing in the follow-up of infantile paralysis.

1916

Miss Edna Braun, after finishing a post-graduate course in obstetrics and executive hospital work, in New York City, is again associated with Dr. William F. Hewitt.

1919

Mabel Pickett's present address is the San Jose Hospital, San Jose, California.

Corena De Jong Hershey is living in Omaha, Nebraska.

Mrs. Florence Willimas Tygett has been traveling in the West with her husband. We are very sorry to learn that their young son, Park, was drowned during the past summer. We wish to extend our sincere sympathy to them.

1920

Mary Billmeyer writes that she is now Department Consultant in Public Health Nursing with the Massachusetts State Department of Public Health Nursing. She is also instructor of school nursing procedures in health, in the Hyannis Normal School.

Elsie Moser is nursing in a refugee hospital in Greece, and as a side line is trying to teach English nursing methods in a Greek training school with no text books to use.

1921

Born to Mr. and Mrs. J. A. Graham (Florence Eckdahl), a John Arthur, Jr., on December 20th.

Born to Mr. and Mrs. R. D. Worling (Lorraine Vickery son, November 7, 1929. The Worling's address is now Imp Bank of India, Fyzabad, U. P., India.

A recent visit was received from Bertha Mann who for s time has been in charge of the nursing at the Tuberculosis Sanitai at Ottawa, Illinois.

The school has been fortunate in having as Health Nurse s September 1st Ella May Van Horn, who brings to us valuable perience gained through Rural Red Cross work as well as the re of extra study in securing her M. S. degree.

1922

Helen Frederick is taking the Public Health Nursing co at the University of Washington.

1923

Mrs. Norma Jernquist Anderson is now in Oakland, Califo

1924

To Dr. and Mrs. G. U. Koivun (Gertrude Farr), a daugl Dorothy Louise, on October 28, 1929.

Married, Della Irene Matthews to Mr. Joseph D. Hayes, Oct 12, 1929.

Married, Lilian Olson to Dr. Ernest S. Olson, June 22, 192

Mrs. Van Gorp (Dorothy Ellis) left her position on the January 1st after six years of valuable service to the school. T who have attended the concerts of the Florence Nightingale ch in recent years will remember Mrs. Van Gorp's poise and management under all conditions. Mr. Van Gorp thinks he made his contribution to nursing progress and has persuaded to use all her abilities in their new home.

Early in January Delia Lampe left for Amherst, Massachu to assist Esther Fairchild, class of 1909, who is in charge of infirmary at Amherst College.

1925

Alma Bratager is with the Scripps Metabolic Clinic, La . California.

Judith Romstad Tanner writes from Proctor, Minneso suburb of Duluth. Mr. Tanner has a pastorate in Proctor.

Dorothy Ainsworth has returned to the school and has on the staff since July, relieving the night supervisors for their n rest, and January 1st assuming the responsible position of tea nursing and doing the follow-up work of the preliminary students on the hospital floors.

Married November 27, 1929, Bonnie May Harper to Dr. Frank Trangmar.

1926

The friends of Irene Gustafson will be sorry to hear that she is a patient at the Edward's Sanitarium, Naperville, Illinois. Write her a letter or, those who can, go to see her.

1928

Ruth Swanson is doing school nursing in Girard, Kansas.

Married, Ellyn Elizabeth Ridley to Mr. James Reeve Stuart, on December 28, 1929.

Married, Genevieve Merriam Borgers to Dr. Clayton F. Hogeboom on December 17, 1928.

The marriage of Katherine D. Stroven to Mr. Zeland R. Holley on December 31, 1929, is announced.

December 16th Alice Spellman after several months' additional experience at Durand Contagious Hospital and in a children's home, was appointed assistant head nurse in the children's department of the hospital, bringing an outside point of view to us.

1929

Married, Ruby Alene Robinson to Dr. E. Elder Freeland, on October 24, 1929, at Waukegan.

Margaret Morgan writes from Topeka, Kansas, that she has charge of a surgical floor at Christ's Hospital and that the hospital is new and beautiful.

LOUIS GEORGEOFF

On November 30th, in the Presbyterian Hospital, after an illness of only a few days, Louis Georgeoff, aged 33, passed away. Louis was born in Bulgaria and came to this country about ten years ago, when he started work in the kitchen of the hospital. After several years in this capacity, he was transferred to the Engineering Department where he was working at the time of his death.

About three years ago Louis took several months' leave of absence and went home to Bulgaria to visit his people. Before returning he married his sweetheart and brought her back with him. They furnished a little home out near Garfield Park and were leading a very industrious and happy life.

Our deep sympathy goes to Mrs. Georgeoff for this great sorrow which she has to bear. We knew the worth of her husband, his loyalty and willingness to render service. He was loved by all his fellows and his loss will be keenly felt.

In Memoriam
1929

The Presbyterian Hospital Bulletin

CHICAGO, ILL. JUNE, 1930 NUMBER 71

Published Quarterly by the Woman's Auxiliary Board. Officers of the Woman's Board: Mrs. C. Frederick Childs, President; Mrs. Clyde E. Shorey, Secretary; Mrs. Frederick R. Baird, Corresponding Secretary; Mrs. William Coggeen, Treasurer; Editor of the Bulletin, Miss Irma Fowler.

Subscriptions, 50 cents a year, may be sent to Asa Bacon, Superintendent, The Presbyterian Hospital of Chicago, or to Mrs. William Coffeen, Hinsdale, Ill., or to Miss Irma Fowler, 209 S. Oak Park Ave., Oak Park.

EDITORIAL

When our thoughts turn from the city this time of year it may be interesting to read of other Presbyterian Hospitals far afield. Perhaps during the summer months you plan a winter vacation and could include a visit to one of the hospitals described in this issue. We hope you will remember to get your jelly glasses and labels before you go away, so that before fall you may accumulate a good supply of delicacies for our hospital shelves. And that you keep in mind the list of books wanted for the Library.

A MODEL HOSPITAL

In a recent trip to Guatemala, Central America, I was much impressed by the splendid work of a missionary hospital in Guatemala City.

The visit to this hospital was one of the objectives of a trip to see all the missionary work under the Presbyterian Board of Foreign Missions in this largest of the five rainbow republics of Central America. Though this Presbyterian Mission work has been established only about 40 years and the force of workers and the equipment have always been painfully inadequate, we found many remarkable results. Missionary work in a country predominately Catholic meets many difficult problems. There are those who feel that missionaries should not be sent to these Latin American countries where Roman Catholicism is so firmly entrenched in the life of the people. It must be remembered, however, that it is the Catholicism of the pre-reformation type and the great mass of the people are ignorant and know so little of their religion that they are entirely untouched by any knoweldege or experience of a religion of the Spirit. Beside this it should be remembered that about half of the people are Indians, to whom the Catholic religion makes little appeal. So there is a wider field of service than any present number of missionaries can cover, among those who are utterly neglected, religiously. There are about 2,200,000 people in Guatemala and half of them are Indians. By far the larger part of all missionary work is done among them. They are said to be the most neglected race, religiously, in the world today. While they are looked down upon by the Spanish and the Ladino class (the Ladino is a mixture of Spanish and Indian), they are considered very promising material if they are given a chance by those who perhaps know them best and who are there to help to give them a "more abundant life."

Through all the years an effort has been made to establish a Christian hospital. In the great earthquake of 1917, when nearly all of the capital city was destroyed, the buildings for missionary work had to be rebuilt along with everything else. Chicago supplied from its missionary resources, at that time, the money to rebuild the girls' school in Guatemala city.

In February, 1922, Dr. Charles A. Ainslie—the son of a missionary home—and his wife, a trained nurse—also from a missionary home—were sent to take charge of what was left of the hospital. At once new life began to be evident. They found very little in buildings or equipment but Dr. Ainslie seems to be as good

4

a business manager as he is a physician and before long he had, by own own effort, gotten as good an operating room as any hospital of its type, with complete modern equipment.

The hospital is not large but it is as large as it can be with only one foreign (American) doctor in charge. It is one story high, built in Spanish style, around a patio—a most lovely place filled with beautiful bright flowers and tropical plants. The whole effect is a delight to see. The rooms are built around the patio, and the view of distant mountains and the loveliness of color all about must help to make the days of suffering more possible for the patients.

There are about 45 beds and there is a daily clinic of 40 to 50 people. Every part of the hospital is in good repair and spotlessly clean and efficiently organized for the best possible results. Every kind of work found in any hospital is here and many other things are done, like the making of the medicines, which can be made cheaper than they can be gotten in any other way. The clinic was one of the most interesting places to see. Early in the morning they begin to arrive—the lame, the halt, the blind. While they wait their turn for attention in a neat, clean white room a sweet faced Bible woman greets them, shows them pictures, gives them leaflets and tells them the story of the gospel. The minister of the beautiful church in the city says that the majority of the people who come into the church come because of the influence and help and spirit of this hospital.

Dr. Ainslie says that "Since the opening of the hospital in 1922, 100,000 consultations and treatments have been given in the clinic. There have been over 5,000 patients in the hospital beds. That means that one out of every 20 who come to the clinic need hospital care. There have been 1,300 major operations, so that one out of four who enter the hospital need operations." The Doctor believes that people appreciate more what they pay for, and so gradually and from very small fees he has built up the hospital funds until it has been possible to do some of the many things which needed to be done. Two residences have been purchased. A large house has been made over into a training school for nurses—the first one in the whole country. An ugly and unkempt vacant lot has been purchased and made into an attractive place for convalescents. A garage has been built for the two hospital cars and the recently acquired ambulance—the gift of a friend. Another doctor is greatly needed for country work. Only about 15 per cent of the people live in the cities and 85 per cent of the native doctors live in the two large cities. They are very anxious to establish a traveling clinic—

with a nurse and a doctor—to go into the country and set up a camp clinic. The camp would be set up near or in a place where Christian work is established and where there is a worker living whom the people know and in whom they have confidence. A week or two would be spent in each place.

Drunkenness is a terrible curse in Guatemala, with all its attendant physical results. There is a site already purchased for a small sanitarium for the tubercular patients in a place suitable for such work.

A word must be said about the fine training school for nurses connected with the hospital. These are two foreign nurses—one in charge—upon whom fall many responsibilities usual and unusual. There is a three-year course of study and training, with about 20 girls—about as many have been graduated, and a wide field of service is open before them. In addition to the usual training every effort is made to surround these girls with wholesome Christian influences and to develop the type of character which is so greatly needed in a country where moral background seems painfully lacking.

When we remember that missionary doctors not only strive to heal the sick, but to teach hygiene and health, to help create a native medical profession, to put nursing on a professional basis and to present the Christian ideal of service, we can begin to appreciate their great task and their sacrificial service. As one thinks of this heroic service, all over the world, of missionary doctors and nurses one is reminded of these words from Ugo Bassi's sermon in a hospital—it was written for patients—but is equally true of those who minister to them:

"Measure thy life by loss instead of gain,
Not by the wine drunk but by the wine poured forth,
For love's strength is in love's sacrifice,
And he who suffers most hath most to give."

—(Mrs. Cleland B.) Harriet B. McAfee.

GANADO HOSPITAL

In the heart of the Navajo Indian reservation, about sixty miles northwest of Gallup, New Mexico, across the Arizona border, is located Ganado Mission and Ganado Hospital. Contrary to often heard statements the American Indian is not decreasing in number but rather increasing at the rate of over ten thousand every decade. Owing to the increase of the Navajo tribe their territory has had to be extended from time to time by executive order until today it covers an area of 23,300,000 acres. Nowhere in this vast region is there a town or village excepting along the Santa Fe railway on the southern border, and these are white man's towns. One can ride across one hundred miles of the Navajo country and scarcely see any sign of human habitation and yet every foot of it is grazed by their flocks and herds. While the Ganado Hospital ministers principally to the Navajo Indians they also take patients from other tribes and have four private rooms for white patients.

In this desert country the Indians' main industry is sheep raising and as it takes from four to twenty acres to feed one sheep, the population is by necessity scattered far and wide over this semi-arid territory. So aside from the hospital in Ganado there are five community centers varying in distance from twelve to seventy miles from Ganado. First aid work is carried on at these out-stations and they act as feeders for the hospital.

The first hospital building was a small adobe one built in 1912. The staff consisted of one doctor and one nurse. On January 23, 1930, the hospital moved into its new home, a fine stone building of seventy-five beds. There is a staff of two doctors and five graduate nurses and they plan to open a nurses' training school in the fall. This new hospital is already outgrown and its capacity will probably have to be doubled next year.

The Indians themselves are keenly interested in the work and when the new X-Ray was purchased, $500 toward the amount required was raised by Indian friends. One day a wealthy old chief brought his son in for examination and before leaving he gave the hospital $500 toward new euqipment. The desert in blossom is a wonderful sight, and when you read of the enthusiasm and spirit of the service of this hospital you feel as if you were witnessing another beautiful form of desert bloom.

HOSPITAL DAY

Hospital Day, Monday, May 12, had a far-spread introduction this year, for on the preceeding Friday night Mr. Bacon spoke over station W.C.F.L. and our Florence Nightingale Chorus sang. Mr. Bacon's speech gives us a concise history of Hospital Day that it would be well to keep in mind. He said, "Next Monday, May 12, is National Hospital Day. The movement which was started ten years ago by Matthew Foley has grown to such proportions that it has come to be known throughout the civilized world. The object of the movement is to encourage the public to visit some hospital on May 12th so that all may become acquainted with the methods of conducting such institutions, their curative, educational and research activities, and also to help win definite support and co-operation from the community."

The Presbyterian Hospital opened its doors that Monday to many visitors who were shown through all departments by competent guides.

THE FLORENCE NIGHTINGALE CONCERT

March 25, 1930, will go down in history as the first day of the most terrific spring blizzard ever experienced in Chicago; and also as the fatal date of the 11th Annual Concert given by Florence Nightingale Chorus of the Presbyterian Hospital School for Nurses!

How utterly helpless we are under weather conditions and how dependent on them for success in any such undertaking, and with brave patience and cheerful courage—how splendidly such obstacles may be overcome!

All these circumstances were illustrated in what occurred on that windy, snowy night, when traffic was almost paralyzed, and even those who most desired to attend were doomed to disappointment. The storm began on Monday night, with rain turning to sleet, which developed later into a heavy snowfall. By noon it seemed to slacken a bit and we hoped might cease by evening, but instead, the elements redoubled their fury, and by night conditions could not have been worse.

The telephone rang all day, bringing many regrets, and numerous dinner parties were canceled. But in spite of wind and weather at 8:15 nearly one hundred persons had gathered in the Crystal

Ballroom, attractively decorated with palms and a gorgeous basket of flowers, kindly donated by Mangel, the florist.

About four hundred tickets for main floor and seventeen boxes had been disposed of, so a fine audience was anticipated; but under the adverse circumstances we were very thankful for those who braved the dangers of coming through the storm—and the others commandeered to fill empty seats from those who were already under the Blackstone roof.

Mr. Arthur Kraft, who had safely arrived from New York to be the welcome soloist, cheered the audience with an extra song while waiting for enough nurses to arrive to begin the program— just one hour after appointed time!

The nurses came in relays in crowded cabs until the last of them took their seats just in time to sing the final group of songs— making sixty in all who finally were gathered on the platform.

Although their songs of Springtime and Lilac Time in Kew Gardens were amusingly inappropriate to the weather, the words were a refreshing reminder of ideal days last May in lovely England.

Mr. Kraft's charming voice was delightfully accompanied by Miss Allum, a friend who had composed and dedicated a song to him and had come just to play that one. And Miss Allum very generously and cleverly filled in all the others for the regular accompaniest, who never arrived.

The nurses looked upon their perilous journeys to and fro as quite an adventure and fortunately no accident occurred nor did anyone take cold—but it was a night of great anxiety for Miss McMillan at the Home—sending them out into the terrible storm— and to Miss Cutler, who, at the other end, had to plan for their transportation back again. It was a great relief when it was safely over and all firmly resolved to take the wise advice of Mr. Carton, president of Men's Hospital Board, never again to plan for a concert in March.

Naturally, with so many friends absent, and expenses unusually heavy (a paid secretary having been found necessary this year, as none of our board members was able to undertake the arduous and detailed clerical work), the receipts were less than usual, but in spite of all complications the Endowment Fund has added nearly $850 to its credit—and the record of a difficult task well accomplished.

Helen V. Drake,
Chairman School of Nursing Committee.

9

ADDRESS TO THE GRADUATING CLASS OF 1930.

Malcolm T. MacEachern, M. D.

This is something of a state occasion, a proper time for ritual, pomp and ceremony. Looking back for a precedent I find there are many aspects of your graduation this evening in common with an ancient ceremony when knighthood was conferred on young men who dedicated their lives to service. Yours is a knighthood of service to humanity. This occasion marks your going forth as apostles of better understanding.

The academic and training years have passed rapidly and I hope pleasantly, filled with wonderful experiences for you. During the early period of your training you progressed through fear control, but after due time you found yourself in the stage of courage control, and finally you enjoyed a self confidence control which has successfully carried you to the goal of your profession. Like the athlete who has been in training and is ready for the scrimmage, your trial period is immediately before you and the real test of what you have acquired lies in how you can apply this knowledge in the best interest of humanity.

This is the season of the year when many nurses emerge into the world of fact. It is not inopportune to extend friendly greetings and congratulations, but, with the reminder that each must become a Columbus, discovering and making a new world for herself. Unlike the ward, the classroom and the laboratory where everything was prepared for you to a great extent, you must expect to encounter difficulties and trials which have to be met and overcome. To the person who has seen fifty years of life "well counted," and to the person who looks at its rosy glamor at twenty-five years there is a vast difference, the person of more years having had the work-a-day experience which is so necessary to complete ordinary book knowledge and apprenticeship.

Education is the preparation of a person to observe accurately, to think clearly, to express comprehensively, to judge soundly, and to act precisely. The education which you have received has not been a mere filler-in of empty spaces of the brain and mind, nor has it been entirely technical. Much, perhaps, did not bear directly on the work of your particular calling or profession, but has been cultural in nature for the preparation of a proper background to make you more capable of observing, thinking, judging and acting for yourself. After all, the best index to education is the degree to which you can measure up to good citizenship.

10

The occasion we celebrate this afternoon is of peculiar interest to all present—

To the members of the graduating classes it means a new commencement in your lives and marks the successful entry into your profession, now throwing out a challenge of service to humanity with its ideals and tradition built up by those who have gone before and which you must perpetuate for those who follow after.

To this fine institution—the Presbyterian Hospital—with its history, tradition and service this event signifies another fine contribution to the welfare of humanity, the relief of suffering and sorrow, the prevention of disease and the promotion of health.

To the community at large this event signifies greater protection and safety for all from ravaging diseases which affect mankind, for surely the influence of these nurses in their respective fields will be for good, and against the enemies—sickness, suffering and the dread monster of death.

There is still a broader interest, that is, the nation at large. Tonight one more unit is added to the great army of health which has made this grand old world safe and beautiful for humanity. Have you ever stopped to think why you are privileged to be here this afternoon under such delightful circumstances? Why are you permitted to enjoy life in this beautiful world? Things have not happened of their own accord; there has been an activating force behind it all. Were it not for the great army of health—doctors, dentists, nurses, dietitians, public health workers, technicians and others maintained and recruited continuously we all would have been wiped out of existence long ago by such dreadful ravaging scourges as bubonic plague, Asiatic cholera, malaria, yellow fever, sleeping sickness, hookworm disease and many others, more fatal than the dread influenza of 1918 and 1919 still fresh in our minds. But through the organized efforts of doctors, nurses, dentists, dietitians and allied groups these diseases have been eliminated or put under control so that the people of this country are safe today. These great accomplishments apply not only to the dread plagues and epidemics, but also to the commoner diseases well known to us. It was with a feeling of seeing something rare and antique when recently in a hospital on the Pacific coast I was shown a case of typhoid fever. Through vaccination, sanitation and education this disease has been placed under subjection and the medical student and nurse-in-training have actually been deprived of sufficient material in our hospitals for adequate observation. As a medical student in 1908, I had access to eight hundred cases for study.

11

Likewise, dipththeria, through toxin-antitoxin, has been reduced to a minimum in many communities, in addition to over eighty per cent reduction in the death rate. Recently in a city within two hundred and fifty miles of here, the Commissioners discussed with me a proposal to use the dipththeria pavilion for other purposes as they had not had a case in the building for over two years, due to the fact that all the children have been immunized.

Diabetes, formerly a fatal disease, accompanied by years of wretchedness, has been placed under control, as you all know, through insulin and diet-therapy. It is good news that the dread disease pernicious anaemia, always fatal, is now being successfully baffled in its ravages and, like diabetes, subject to control. This is due to the efforts of scientific workers as Minet, Boston; Sturgen, Ann Arbor; Whipple, Rochester, New York, and others.

You are all aware that hydrophobia or rabies and smallpox have been conquered in their ravages of human life, and any person dying from the latter today could reasonably be accused of suicide.

It gives us all a measure of comfort and joy when we realize the average life of man has advanced from forty to fifty-eight years during the past three or four decades, and concurrent with this has been a drop in the average mortality of the United States from twenty-two per thousand to ten or even less in some communities. A recent noted surgeon stated that the mortality following major surgery had dropped from eighteen to three per cent during the past twelve to fifteen years in well conducted hospitals and clinics. We know that the average days' stay of patients in hospitals has been cut in two, and even less in some cases, and, at the same time, the mortality rate has dropped accordingly.

These are good tidings! There has been a far-reaching force behind all this, a great army of health—doctors, dentists, nurses, dietitians and allied groups with hospitals, laboratories and other means effectively battling with these diseases. It is this great army which has given the world its real protection and to which one more unit will be officially added tonight to assure greater safety to the nation.

While much has been accomplished there is still much to do. Many of the common diseases must be placed under greater control. The five great enemies to the human race are still rampant. I refer particularly to:

(a) Diseases of the heart—with 186 deaths annually per 100,000 population.

(b) Diseases of the kidney—with 96 deaths annually per 100,000 population.

12

(c) Cancer—with 93 deaths annually per 100,000 population.
(d) Tuberculosis—with 86 deaths annually 100,000 population.
(e) Arteriosclerosis—with 84 deaths annually per 100,000 population.

Doctors, dentists, nurses and dietitians must continue to battle with these diseases and help prevent their ravages. Yours is one of great opportunity for service to mankind.

What have you gained in your years of study and training? Let us take a brief inventory of a few of the most outstanding requirements:

(a) *Knowledge*—You have acquired an extensive social and technical knowledge which prepares you to undertake your professional activities. This knowledge is yours and no one can take it from you. They may rob you of your money, jewels or other worldly possessions, but they cannot take this knowledge. It is, indeed, a great heritage from your Alma Mater.

(b) *Trained Mind*—You have acquired a better trained mind—trained to think better, to evaluate, to discriminate and to act. This has followed through the proper assimilation of cultural and technical knowledge. Your presence here as participants in the graduation exercises is a testimonial to the fact that this assimilation has been accomplished. Again you are under everlasting obligation to your great Alma Mater.

(c) *Qualities of Character*—Education such as you have had cannot but mould character and develop the higher qualities which go to make the content of efficient and worthy workers and good citizenship. You have all come in close contact with human life with its peculiarities and eccentricities, its joys and its sorrows, its successes and its failures, and I am sure this has taught you to be human, kind, sympathetic, honest and optimistic, and to take the bitter with the sweet with a glad and cheerful heart.

(d) *Qualities of Personality*—Most of you, and, in fact, all of you, have intimate contact with the patient in the practice of your profession. In this contact you must do more than observe, examine, order and treat in the technical sense. You must radiate something intangible from your personality which will give the patient mental ease and comfort as well as better adaptation to his or her surroundings and thus take treatment better. This something cannot be described, but is well illustrated in what the English soldier wounded in Alma wrote from the Barracks Hospital, Scutari, in 1855, regarding Florence Nightingale: "What a comfort it was to see her pass; she would speak to one and nod and smile to many more. She

13

could not do it all, you know; we lay there by hundreds, but we could kiss her shadow as it fell and lay our heads on the pillow again, content." This is essential to success in your profession.

You have heard a good deal, I am sure, regarding ethics during your course of study. Too much cannot be said in an appeal for strict adherence to the Code of Ethics of your profession. The imminent danger at present is the tendency of some nurses to serve in their professional capacity in the environment of irregular or unethical practice of medicine. Nurses should only work in the environment of regular ethical or scientific medicine.

Could I but speak the mind of your beloved Alma Mater and this audience I know they would like to exhort you to develop leadership, render good service, continually advance your knowledge and maintain youth for all time in your professional career. Leadership may be latent or dormant in many often precipitated accidentally or incidentally.

Fortunately for us neither wealth nor books can exclusively solve the riddle of a successful career. Work, and plenty of it, is needed, coupled with good service. You have been provided with the means of utilizing science and good will to make life worth living for every man, woman and child. In the practice of your profession "Service, Not Self," should be your motto.

A good doctor, a good dentist, a good nurse, or a good dietitian must never close their books. You must always be good students; advance your knowledge, not only through daily experience but by reading, observation, travel and post-graduate courses. Each day you must add to, replace, or readjust the knowledge acquired. Remember that well guided, sound experience is the best teacher.

Maintain your youth—that kind of youth which in the words of an anonymous writer is described as follows:

"Youth is not a time of life. It is a state of mind. It is not a matter of ripe cheeks, red lips and supple knees.

It is a temper of the will, a quality of the imagination, a vigor of the emotions. Youth means a temperamental predominance of courage over timidity, of the appetite of adventure over the love of ease. This often exists in a man of 50 or more than in a youth of 20. Nobody grows old by merely living a number of years. People grow old only by deserting their ideals. Years wrinkle the skin, but to give up enthusiasm wrinkles the soul.

Worry, doubt, self-distrust, fear and despair—these are the long years that bow the head and turn the growing spirit back to

14

dust. You are as young as your self-confidence, as old as your fear; as young as your hope, as old as your despair.

In the central place of your heart there is a wireless station: so long as it receives messages of beauty, hope, cheer, grandeur, courage and power from the earth, from man and from the infinite, so long are you young. When the wires are all down and all the central place of your heart is covered with the snows of pessimism and the ice of cynicism, then are you grown old indeed, and may God have mercy on your soul."

Your future is just as beautiful and interesting as you make it. Sometimes you may be discouraged; sometimes you may feel it is not worth while, but always remember it is a great privilege to serve at the altar of science. The beauty of your work is well described in the word portrait of the doctor and the nurse when the author penned the following lines:

You must lighten the load of human sorrow.

You must dispel or diminish the gloom of the sick chamber.

You must take the bitter with the sweet, and all with a cheerful heart.

You must treat the social ills of the heart and mind of the patient and replace these with comfort and contentedness.

You must pluck from the pillow of pain its thorn and make the hard couch soft with poppies of delicious rest.

You must let the light of joy in dark and desolate dwellings.

You must rekindle the lamp of hope in the bosom of despair.

You must call back the radiance of the lusterless eye and the bloom of the fading cheek.

You must send new vigor through failing limbs.

And finally, when exhausted in all other resources and baffled in your skill, you must blunt the arrows of death and render less rugged and precipitious the inevitable pathway to the tomb.

Surely it is a high calling for you to serve at the altar of the science and art of nursing.

GROUP NURSING IN NEW YORK

Group nursing units form a striking feature of the proposed Gotham Hospital buildings soon to be erected in New York City. This, it is believed, will be the first hospital in New York designed particularly to meet the needs of the middle-salaried class.

Each of the group nursing units, according to the plans which have been approved by the board of directors, will be a small hospital in itself with four private rooms opening out of a private corridor in the center of which a nurse's desk and supply base will be placed. With each unit will go two utility rooms. Thus one nurse can attend several patients, the number depending on the seriousness of their condition.

"In all," states *The Evening World* of March 22, "there will be 219 beds with 50 private rooms available under the endowment plan at $5 a day; 50 semi-private at $4; and 50 beds in small wards at $3. About 50 beds will be reserved for patients able to pay full hospital rates."

AND IN THE HOME

The need for small-package nursing in the home was voiced at the recent Institute for State Executive Secretaries, by Olive Sewell, of Michigan, who said, "The questions as to where and how hourly nursing should be conducted will solve themselves in time. The most important point is that we are thinking and talking hourly nursing."

HOURLY NURSING SERVICE

Nursing service by the hour by graduate registered nurses is now available for patients in their homes. Recommended for cases of illness where full time nursing service is not required.

SERVICE CHARGES FOR HOURLY NURSING

$2.00 for the first hour or fraction thereof.
$1.00 for the second hour or fraction thereof.
Service limited to three hours per visit, between the hours of 8:30 A. M. to 10 P. M.

Send Calls to
The Chicago Nurses' Club and Registry

116 South Michigan Avenue   Chicago, Illinois
Telephone State 8542

Endorsed by Central Council for Nursing Education, and The First District of the Illinois State Association of Graduate Nurses

The library will appreciate donations of good books on any of the following subjects. A few examples of titles are listed, but other standard works are just as acceptable.

HISTORY AND POLITICS

Davis—History of France.

Basset—Short History of the U. S.

Bryce—American Commonwealth.

Breasted—Ancient Times.

Beard—American Government and Politics

Hazen—Europe Since 1815.

BIOGRAPHY.

TRAVEL.

ESSAYS.

PHILOSOPHY.

POETRY—(Especially collections by various authors).

PLAYS.

ARTS—(Painting, Sculpturing, Music, Household Decorations, etc.)

SCIENCE—(Astronomy, Geology, Nature, etc.)

STANDARD FICTION—(Not only American, but also English. Russian, French, and Scandinavian translations.)

FREE BEDS AND MEMBERS

A donation of $50,000 entitles the donor to name a twelve-bed ward, which shall remain as a perpetual memorial to the donor, or any other individual he wishes.

A donation of $20,000 carries the same privileges for a four or six bed ward.

A donation of $10,000 entitles the donor to designate a room in the Private Pavilion which shall be named as desired by the donor and remain as a perpetual memorial.

A donation of $7,500 designates a bed in perpetuity.

A donation of $5,000 designates a bed during one life.

A donation of $5,000 designates a bed in the Children's Ward in perpetuity.

A donation of $300 annually designates a free bed in the general wards.

A donation of $100 or more constitutes the donor a life member of the institution.

A yearly donation of $10 constitutes an annual member.

FORM OF BEQUEST

I give and bequeath to the Presbyterian Hospital of the City of Chicago, incorporated under the law of the State of Illinois, the sum of ....Dollars to be applied to the use and benefit of the said hospital, under the direction of the managers thereof.

FORM OF DEVISE

I give and devise to the Presbyterian Hospital of the City of Chicago, incorporated under the law of the State of Illinois, all that, etc. [*describe the property*], to be had and holden to the said the Presbyterian Hospital of the City of Chicago, and their successors and assigns, for the use and benefit of the said hospital.

ALUMNÆ NOTES

ENDOWMENT

The Endowment Committee, Jane High, 1924 Chairman, has new plans for raising money this year and the Bazaar will be omitted. The Alumnæ in and near Chicago gave a subscription dance May 23 in the Crystal Ballroom of the Blackstone Hotel; this event closing the week of graduation festivities. Much interest was displayed and the returns were very gratifying. The committee realized one thousand ninety dollars from the sale of tickets, which will net about eight hundred dollars for the Endowment Fund.

It is hoped that every alumna on reading this will look about in her own community; that these groups will come together and devise some method of raising money for the Endowment Fund. The committee would like the various amounts raised to be sent in to Jane High, 1750 W. Congress Street, by December 1, 1930.

This year's proceeds from the Rummage Sale, to be held in the fall, will be used for our Sick Benefit and Relief Fund, which has but $300.60. Please send anything you may have to the school. Miss Aylward will give us storage space.

Arrangements are being made by Doris Kerwin, 1921, for a Presbyterian reunion dinner on Monday or Wednesday evening during the A. N. A. Biennial Convention in Milwaukee, June 9 to 14. Please see her as soon as you arrive.

We want to remind you of Home Coming as usual on November 11. Plan your trips to Chicago over that date.

1906

Judith Alice Gerrish has been in Tucson, Arizona, this winter and spring, engaged in nursing work. She also writes of having seen Winifred McLeod, who has spent the winter in Phoenix, Arizona.

1908

Peninal K. Jones stopped over to call on us one day in April en route from California to New York City. Her plans are thence on to Europe to do some sight-seeing, terminating her trip at the American Hospital in Paris to do some nursing work.

1909

Alma E. Forester, supervisor of Public Health Nursing Service, Racine Chapter, American Red Cross, Racine, Wisconsin, finds the work there very interesting and full of possibilities.

1911

Hilda Johnson Anguin is happy in her nursing work at Santa Barbara, Calif.

1912

Sarah A. Crosby is now engaged in nursing work at Abernchill, North Fork, Virginia.

1914

The summer session at the University of Minnesota School of Nursing and Department of Preventive Medicine and Public Health includes two of our graduates on its teaching staff; Miss Eula Butzerin (1914 Assistant Professor of Preventive Medicine and Public Health and Director of the Course on Public Health Nursing (U. of Minnesota); also Miss Elnora E. Thomson (1909) Director of the Course in Public Health Nursing, Professor of Applied Sociology, Portland School of Social Work, University of Oregon.

1916

Verda Hickcox is in Bankok, Siam, with Mildred Porter, 1925. They are establishing a hospital and maternity service under the Rockefeller Foundation. Miss Porter is Director of Nursing and Miss Hickcox, after a six months' course in midwifery in London, is teaching it to the native women. Miss Porter and Miss Hickcox were presented to the King and Queen of Siam recently, following the opening of the new hospital.

Mary Ruggles Banks and her husband are in the Ural Mountains, Russia. Mr. Banks is a mining engineer.

1918

A visit from Mrs. E. L. Hart (Camilla Harper) who lives in Red Bluff, Calif. Mrs. Hart, a director of a health camp, is interested in developing public health nursing in her locality and is doing her best to make use of her professional knowledge.

1919

Miss Lelind Townsend has done some very interesting work at the Neurological Institute this winter, particularly along the line of a series of lectures in neurology for the special nurses. The lectures were given by different members of the medical staff, with an average of 200.

1921

Miss Dorothea Jackson is enjoying her work with the School of Nursing Department of the City of Detroit, where she has been since February of this year.

A letter has been received from Anna Rauch MacKenzie in the Orange Free State, South Africa. She and her husband live on a 6,000-acre sheep ranch.

Mary E. Bricker, who is at home after a five year period of missionary service in India, does not expect to return this fall. During the past year she has been enrolled at Western Reserve University School of Public Health Nursing and has found it most profitable and enjoyable.

A letter from Camille Blair states that she is well on her third year's service in the Army Nurse Corps of Fitzsimmons, Colorado. She is also planning on attending the University of Washington next fall to take a public health course of one year.

Louise A. Simmons Schneider and Louise Bartholomaus (1927) are also planning trips to Europe this summer and expect to make the American Hospital, Paris, their destination for a while.

1922

Mildred Lunde has returned to New York City and is superintendent of Nurses at Riverside Hospital, one of New York's communicable disease hospitals.

Ruth TeLinde is now one of the assistant supervisors at one of the Henry Street offices (New York City). She is to represent Henry Street at the Biennial Convention at Milwaukee in June and is to read a paper there.

1923

Margaret Mosiman received a Ph.B. degree from the University of Chicago this spring. She has been appointed to attend a seminar in Mexico during July.

Mrs. C. W. Patterson (Lillian B. Patterson) is planning to take some public health nursing work at the University of Washington, Seattle, this summer.

From Sanjan, Thana District, India, comes a very interesting letter from Isla F. Knight. She seems very proud of her dispensary, which has been open about one year. She has two Mohammedan children that she is supporting, one a boy of eleven years, the other a baby who was abandoned when one day old and brought to the hospital by the police. Miss Knight expects to return to the United States next summer and while here is planning to take a course in midwifery as that seems to be a woman's work in India.

The hospital has again been most fortunate in that it has been made possible to add a second endowed day nurse—the Ernest A. Hamill Nurse—Miss Orizaba Frye, who for a number of years has been the Gladys Foster night nurse is the first one to hold this position.

Miss Nora Ziebell (1924) has taken the position left vacant by Miss Frye, while Miss Flora Schrankel (1923) is the assistant night superintendent.

1924

We congratulate Miss Edwina MacDougall on being one of the recipients of the Isabelle Hampton Robb scholarship. She expects to attend Columbia University.

Mary M. Anderson, Rochester General Hospital, Rochester, N. Y., as president of the League of Nursing Education, also a member of the official Registry Committee, is doing some very interesting work. They are planning to have an institute this summer and also have started a special finance committee to raise money for the purpose of sending delegates to the national convention at Milwaukee, in June.

Miss Delia Lampe writes that she is doing floor duty at the Presbyterian Hospital, New York City, and finds her work and New York most interesting.

Gertrude Sturgess spent part of January 11th at the Sprague Home. Since graduating, Miss Sturgess has held a hospital head nurseship, and secured her A.B. degree at Columbia. Also, she has had a year's experience with the New York City Maternity Teaching Center, some months work in teaching mothers in the Brooklyn Dispensary clinics and is now associated with Dr. Frank E. Abbott of Indianapolis, her home town, in an endeavor to introduce prenatal and post natal teaching into that city. This is an example of how some of our graduates are making a valuable contribution to their home communities.

1925

From Hot Lake, Oregon, Ida Saari Phy, comes news as to the progress of nursing organization there. They are planning to organize a District Nurses' Registry, also by July 1st all nurses engaged in nursing work in the State of Oregon must be registered in that state.

1926

Sylvia Melby is now assistant superintendent of nurses at Anker Hospital, St. Paul.

Maxine Day is with the Boyd Company Health Department, Ashland, Kentucky.

1927

Helen McCuish Oltman and her husband and baby leave this fall for the mission field in Amoy, China.

Miss Edna Quigley and Miss Byrdette Roemer, having motored to California this spring, are now employed in California hospitals—Miss Quigley as assistant night supervisor at the Good Samaritan Hospital, Los Angeles; while Miss Roemer is on night duty at the Hollywood Hospital.

1928

Such an interesting, enthusiastic letter has been received from Lillian M. Young from Zululand, So. Africa.

Ruth Swanson, who has been school nurse at Girard, Kansas, the past year, is contemplating on taking a course in public health at the University of Chicago this summer.

1929

Esther Severance is now a member of the nursing staff of the Pediatric Unit of the Barnes Hospital, St. Louis.

Esther Matthews has accepted an industrial position at Mason City, Iowa, with the J. B. Decker Packing Company.

Miss Madeline Swetland is now at the Toledo Hospital, Toledo, Ohio, as nursing supervisor and assistant head nurse in the maternity department.

Miss Alice Burgheer is to be assistant superintendent of nurses, Park Hospital Clinic, Mason City, Iowa.

MARRIAGES

Margaret Evelyn Gottfried, 1919, married to Mr. Carl A. Menchhofer, Jan. 13, 1930, at Lima, Ohio.

Ruth Smallegan, 1925, married to Mr. Richard Alexander, April, 1930, at Forest Grove, Michigan.

BIRTHS

Mr. and Mrs. Sidney Owen (Clara Peterson, 1925), a son, Sidney, Jr., February 12, 1930.

Dr. and Mrs. William Steele (Anne Patterson, 1926), a daughter, Roberta Anne, April 13, 1930.

Dr. and Mrs. Donald C. Mower (Velna Pickard, 1925), a son, Robert, February 19, 1930.

Reverend and Mrs. J. O. Jovaag (Pearl Martinson, 1926), a son, Harold SeVir, March 19, 1930.

Mr. and Mrs. F. Willard Cook (Eleanor Severin, 1927), a son, Kenneth Severin, April 22, 1930.

Mr. and Mrs. Milton Olsen (Lenore Stillman, 1922), a son, Robert William, February 5, 1930.

ALUMNÆ OPEN MEETING FOR THE GRADUATING CLASS

The annual Open Meeting and Tea given to the graduating class of 1930 was held at Sprague Home on Friday afternoon, April 11th.

The meeting opened with a short business session presided over by Miss Cooper, President of the Association. Reports were given of the work this year, plans suggested for the Annual Luncheon and the next regular meeting.

Miss Jessie Stevenson of the Visiting Nurses' Association told us clearly about the various nursing organizations, particularly the First District, the State, the National Associations and the League of Nursing Education. She explained what could be gained by supporting these. Miss Desse Greek reviewed our own special Alumnæ interests; the Alumnæ itself and its aims, the Endowment Fund, its accomplishments and future plans; the Mary Byrne Fund; and the Gladys Foster Fund.

We were especially privileged to have with us Miss Edna Burgess on furlough from her mission in Tabriz, Persia. Miss Burgess has spoken at several previous meetings, but as time was limited she could not tell the graduates as much as she would have, nor as much as they would have liked to know. What she did say was intensely interesting.

Feature dancing by several children from a dancing school amused and entertained us for a short time before tea. The tea tables were gay with bright spring flowers and our treasured anniversary silver. Tea, delicious sandwiches and cakes were served. Every one enjoyed meeting the members of the graduating class and greeting friends. We departed hoping for many more such occasions and wishing the graduating class all success.

MAY 2, 1930

The Junior B's turned the annual tea for the seniors into a bridge this year. From the minute one stepped into the assembly room at the Sprague Home, with its mellow lighting of gay bridge lamps, the party was a success. The brisk playing ended with prizes (exquisite silhouettes and dainty book ends) and a hilarious scramble for front seats to hear and see Mr. Froseth, the famous magician. Believe it or not, he showed us exactly how to transfer a scarlet silk handkerchief through air from glass to egg shell—and then broke an honest-to-goodness egg from the same shell! We unanimously invited him to lunch with us on delicious chicken salad and strawberry tarts.

MARY PORTZLINE.

Each year the graduating classes of the nursing schools from the hospitals of this vicinity join in attending a combined Baccalaureate service at the St. Paul Methodist Church.

This year the date was May 18th and each school marched up the aisle in processional promptly at 7:30 p. m. We were very fortunate in having for the speaker Dr. A. S. Moore, Superintendent of the Chicago District of the Methodist Church. He took for his subject, "Ministering to Our Life's Hungers," a message well worth while.

Several delightful numbers were given by the chorus of the Cook County Hospital, School of Nursing.

The graduating classes thoroughly appreciated the warm reception given them and the feeling of unity brought about by the four schools sharing in the one service.

JESSE TULLOCH.

GIFTS FROM THE GRADUATING CLASS

This year, A Division of the 1930 class combined with the B 1929 Division and presented the school with a radio. It was installed in the assembly room at Christmas time and has been a most busy radio—giving much pleasure to all members of the household.

On graduating day, B Division of the 1930 class brought its carefully thought-out gifts, which were on display on the first floor for the afternoon. By this contribution students now in the school, when using the roof for informal affairs or for Sunday breakfasts, will no longer lack a coffee percolator, a waffle iron, toaster—and luxury of luxury—a popcorn toaster, all electric.

We are beginning to believe, with all these gifts arriving, that even the preliminary class promise of producing an airplane when they graduate may come true.

The Graduating Exercises of the School of Nursing of Presbyterian Hospital were held at the Sprague Home on Thursday, May 22nd.

The address was given by Doctor Malcom T. Mac Eachern, Director of Hospital Activities, American College of Surgeons. Following the address, the graduating class was presented to the Board of Managers by Miss McMillan. Mr. Alfred T. Carton, President of the Board, conferred the diplomas upon fifty-eight students. The

25

school pins were presented by Mrs. C. Frederick Childs, President of the Women's Board.

A delightful feature of the afternoon was the singing of two groups of songs by the Florence Nightingale Chorus.

After the services tea was served to the graduating class and to the guests.

The A Division of the graduating class was most delightfully entertained on April 25th by the Senior B's at a tea in the Narcissus Room at Marshall Field's. This has been the custom through the past several years and is anticipated with pleasure.

The dainty service and low, sweet music created that harmonious atmosphere which helped to make this a most enjoyable occasion.

RUTH MOON.

The Alumnæ Association held their annual luncheon in honor of the graduating classes on the afternoon of Friday, May 23, in the Crystal Ballroom of the Blackstone.

Miss Florence Cooper, President of the Assoication, introduced the speakers. Miss McMillan told us of several of the "family" who were working abroad or working in specialized fields. Mrs. Graham, of the Women's Board, spoke a few words stressing the importance of informing the public as to the meaning of modern scientific nursing. Mrs. Irons told us how much she enjoyed being associated with the Alumnæ. Miss Dorothy Heffner and Miss Myrtle Vandermeulen, representing the graduating classes, thanked the Alumnæ for the delightful event.

Everyone enjoyed the charming singing of Eva Gordon Horadesky, who entertained with a well-chosen group of songs.

RUTH SPERLING.

In Memoriam

JESSIE BREEZE

January 15, 1864.   March 23, 1930

A brief memorial service for Miss Breeze was held at the April meeting of the Woman's Board. The words of Mrs. Childs, who presided, of Mrs. Bass, Dr. Gregg and Mrs. Penfield brought out the affectionate, understanding relationship between the Board and Miss Breeze as head of our Social Service Department, her value as a friend, her wonderful spirit of service and her firmness of character with its leaven of abundant humor. She was a beloved figure to all of us as she stood before us telling of the finely constructive work of her department.

Speaking for the nurses, Miss McMillan said: "We feel in the hospital that we have lost a good friend who was ready at all times to help in each of our undertakings.

"Nothing that the nursing group ventured upon was uninteresting to Miss Breeze and she was invariably among the first to purchase tickets and make a contribution to every cause.

"In her last illness she was an example of courage to all who saw her. To the very end she was glad to hear of other peoples problems, to help them when possible, to enjoy a story and appreciative always of everything done for her.

"One side of Miss Breeze which may be unknown to this group was the fact of her large number of close friends, some of them of long years' standing, who knew and valued her loyalty, her good judgment and clear headedness.

"The members of her own Alumnæ Association listened with respect to her advice regarding policies and selected her to represent them on the Board of the Illinois Training School, of which she was an active member at the time of its disbandment in 1929.

"Fortune was not propitious to Miss Breeze, her whole life apparently being a sacrifice for others. On her burial day even the weather could not be kind, but prohibited her friends showing the last evidences of friendship.

"Nothing, however, can shut out the spirit and courage of her life from those who knew her."

For the hospital, Mr. Bacon said: "It has been said that it is possible to do Social Service work and not be a Christian. I, for one, do not believe that is so. We are all members of a society which is not complete until the sacredness of each personality is recognized and given proper scope. Whether conscious of it or not, Social Service is doing this.

"Miss Breeze's generosity was not the indiscriminate type which is stirred to action by a picture of extreme misery. To her every individual was of supreme worth, not only to God himself, but to society. Therefore all these many years she has given of herself freely in her effort to help mankind. Her sacrifice has stimulated us. Miss Breeze was, and her memory will continue to be, an inspiration not only to her co-workers here in the hospital but to the community at large.

FROM THE ILLINOIS TRAINING SCHOOL ALUMNÆ REPORT—
APRIL, 1930

At the age of twenty-one Miss Breeze entered the Illinois Training School for Nurses, completing her course in 1887, in the fifth class graduating from the school.

For a few years after graduation she did private duty nursing. As a result of her keen interest in every phase of knowledge concerning health and disease she sought in the Women's Medical College more adequate preparation for the most intelligent type of service in her chosen field and was a student there during one year.

In 1893 she was called to her Alma Mater where for ten years her inspiring, stimulating, refining personality left an indelible impression upon patients, medical staff, faculty and student nurses. Whether serving on the nurses directory, as teacher, as supervisor or as assistant superintendent of nurses she gave of herself faithfully, unstintingly, joyously. Her wonderful grasp of details, her remarkable sense of justice, her clairvoyant insight, her keen sense of humor, her fine art of teaching, her sympathetic understanding, made her admired, respected, feared and loved by her hosts of loyal students.

After a much needed rest in 1903 in the home of the McIsaac sisters, her close friends and co-workers in the Training School for many years, she again entered the field of private duty nursing. Her rare personality became a benediction in the Isham home during the evening of life for the mother there.

After finishing her duties there she entered the School of Civics and Philanthropy of the University of Chicago and in 1912 was appointed organizer and director of the Social Service Department of the Presbyterian Hospital of Chicago, the position she filled so eminently up to near the time of her death. To this work she carried rare judgment, discretion, sympathy, understanding and experience, with untiring energy and devotion to the welfare of those who needed council or help.

Miss Breeze was a charter member and the first secretary of the I. T. S. Alumnæ Association, organized September 3, 1891. She held various offices in the organization and always was active in the promotion of its varied interests. One concern uppermost in her mind during recent months was the welfare of those life-long sister workers whose devoted, unselfish service may have made it impossible for them to provide for the evening of life. It was her earnest desire that the Alumnæ funds be wisely directed in channels of helpfulness for our worthy women who have so richly earned the just rewards of the faithful—freedom from fear of the hazards of old age and illness.

Her generous bequests to our endowed bed fund, to the American Nurses' Relief Fund and to the Presbyterian Hospital are lasting memorials to her vital interest in the relief of human suffering.

In 1911 she was elected to membership on the Board of Directors of the Illinois Training School for Nurses, an honor never before conferred upon a member of the Alumnæ. With her rare qualities of mind and heart and with her rich background of experience and understanding of the problems of the training school and of the needs of the student nurse, her clear judgment and wise council were a constant source of strength in that body. She was recognized as a most valuable member of this group with whom she served efficiently and faithfully up to the close of its work.

To no other person has it been given to promote the interests of our school so directly and loyally throughout its long and honorable history, and no one has left a finer imprint of high ideals of service upon the hearts of her students than has Jessie Breeze.

Throughout her professional life she maintained an ideal home for her loved ones—mother, grandmother and widowed invalid sister's family. Home meant much to her. In her bright, characteristic way she said to a young nurse who was to leave her chosen profession to care for an invalid mother: *"Remember* that there is nothing more worth while than making a real home." Her devotion to her dear ones was a joyous *giving* of *herself* which was to her the meaning of life in all her human relations.

During her long and painful illness there were no complaints. Her heroic courage, her infinite patience, the power of the mind over the body, her brave forgetfulness of self, her constant thoughtfulness of others, her active interest in her friends and in affairs of the world, her characteristic bright conservation and her never failing

sense of humor, can never be forgotten by those who were privileged
to enter her blossoming shrine during her closing days.

"O may I join that choir invisible
Of those immortal dead who live again
In minds made better by their presence: live
In pulses stirred to generosity,
In deeds of daring rectitude, in scorn
For miserable aims that end with self,
In thoughts sublime that pierce the night like stars,
And with their mild persistence urge man's search
To vaster issues."

CHARLOTTE JOHNSON, '03·

31

THE SPRAGUE HOME
Nurses' Residence, 1750 West Congress Street

The Presbyterian Hospital Bulletin

CHICAGO, ILL.   NOVEMBER, 1930   NUMBER 72

Published Quarterly by the Woman's Auxiliary Board. Officers of the Woman's Board: Mrs. C. Frederick Childs, President; Mrs. Clyde E. Shorey, Secretary; Mrs. Frederick R. Baird, Corresponding Secretary; Mrs. Edward L. Beatie, Treasurer; Editor of the Bulletin, Miss Irma Fowler.

Subscriptions, 50 Cents a Year, may be sent to Asa Bacon, Superintendent, The Presbyterian Hospital of Chicago, or to Miss Irma Fowler, 209 South Oak Park Avenue, Oak Park

EDITORIAL

Forward through the ages
  In unbroken line,
Move the faithful spirits
  At the call divine;
Gifts in differing measure,
  Hearts of one accord,
Manifold the service
  One the sure reward.

Wider grows the kingdom,
  Reign of love and light;
For it we must labor
  Till our faith is sight;
Prophets have proclaimed it,
  Martyrs testified,
Poets sung its glory,
  Heroes for it died.

Not alone we conquer,
  Not alone we fall;
In each loss or triumph
  Lose or triumph all.
Bound by God's far purpose
  In our living whole,
Move we on together
  To the shining goal.
        —Hymn, "Forward Through the Ages."

An old missionary hymn written of those who went out to serve, but surely just as applicable to those who serve through our hospital. And it is well worth while to learn what the hospital accomplishes as a missionary enterprise. Did you know that in the first nine months of this year the Presbyterian Hospital has done charity work amounting to $140,000? Every religion was represented among the patients, every state in the Union and forty-seven foreign countries.

3

PARAGRAPHS FROM THE 1930 MEETING OF THE AMERICAN HOSPITAL ASSOCIATION AT NEW ORLEANS

Southern hospitality, that wonderful quality that is so often referred to in the North, was actually on display in all of its varied forms at the New Orleans meeting of the American Hospital Association and the meetings of allied associations held October 20 to 24. The attendance at the meeting was larger than was expected by even the most optimistic and the program which on paper shaped up well proved to be even better than it read. Dr. Bert W. Caldwell, executive secretary of the American Hospital Association, reported that there were more hospitals represented at the meeting than had been the case for several years past and that there were fewer disappointments from people who had been assigned places on the various round tables and at the sessions.

Business, politics, pseudopolitics, social activities and excellently attended sectional meetings were the order of the week in the South. Paul H. Fesler, superintendent, University of Minnesota Hospital, Minneapolis, was elected president; Asa S. Bacon, superintendent, Presbyterian Hospital, Chicago, was reelected treasurer.

FROM THE ADDRESS OF THE PRESIDENT, CHRISTOPHER G. PARNALL, M. D., ROCHESTER, N. Y.

The last meeting of the American Hospital Association a year ago last June was particularly notable because it was held in conjunction with the first International Hospital Congress. An unusual opportunity was provided for hospital workers from all over the world to learn something of each others' methods and problems. The next congress will be held in Vienna in June, 1931, and it promises to be a landmark in the history of the hospital movement throughout the world. The influence of this association is not confined to the countries its membership includes but reaches literally every section of the globe. A great responsibility rests with us to exercise the highest type of leadership and I am sure that we shall not fail to respond to the challenge.

There is a great need for public education concerning hospital service and all it embraces. The lamentable lack of knowledge of the average citizen of what the hospital is doing and what it stands for is the greatest obstacle to hospital progress. The public is suspicious of the hospital and the suspicion is almost entirely based on ignorance of the problems the hospital must face. Dispel this ignorance and hospitals deserving public support and encouragement will receive it in unstinted measure, and those whose conduct does not entitle them to consideration will either have to raise their standards or close their doors.

THE EVER RECURRING QUESTIONS OF COSTS

Perhaps no problem connected with the care of the sick has received so much public attention as the alleged high cost of hospital and medical service. Indeed the cost seems to cause more public agitation than the question of whether or not people are getting what they pay for. There are kinds of hospital and medical service that are costly at any price; on the other hand, if skillful treatment and good care mean restoration to health and happiness, the service may be worth anything it costs. The cost of a necessary and an unnecessary operation may be the same. There is a vast difference in the value. Generally speaking, it is unquestionably true that judged by results the value of medical service and hospital care has increased faster than has the cost.

It is to be regretted that many more hospital trustees are not members of this association and that they are not present at these important conclaves, which offer such convenient opportunities for acquiring information in every branch of hospital activity. I believe if every hospital trustee who regarded his position as a serious trust could clearly understand its advantages, both to himself and to his hospital, he would obtain membership in the American Hospital Association. That there is an increasing interest on the part of members of hospital boards in the association and its work is an encouraging omen.

Offering tremendous possibilities for usefulness are: the classification, examination and approval of equipment and supplies so that certification of the American Hospital Association would assure merchandise meeting definite standards; investigation of methods and procedures in hospitals; the keeping of records and accounts; advice and consultation on building programs and equipment of buildings; advice on matters pertaining to hospital management; community relationships; service to personal members in the many problems that constantly arise; working out definite and practical relationships with other organizations; participation in the program of hospital standardization with various public and private agencies in a multitude of activities which directly or indirectly concern the hospitals. There seems to be no limit to the possible usefulness of the association. There is a limit, however, a very definite one, to the actual service. the association can render, both to its institutional and to its personal members and hospitals outside its membership.

Our whole problem can be summed up in one word: money. We already have a large percentage of the possible total institutional membership, and the personal membership is a relatively small body composed largely of. those who can pay only nominal dues. We have about reached the limit of our income from membership. Our resources are expressed in thousands; our legitimate needs, if we cover the field of hospital service adequately, can almost be stated without extravagance in millions. Where such tangible and legitimate needs exist, there are always ways to meet them. We must direct our attention to securing from those who desire to be of great service and who have the means to satisfy their desires, sufficient income so that the association can enter a new period of enormous usefulness not only to its members but, indeed, to the hospitals of the world.

FROM OTHER SPEAKERS

At a public session of the trustees' section held on Tuesday night Dr. Stewart R. Roberts, of Atlanta, Georgia, spoke on "Multiple Cares and Costs." Medicine as a social service to the whole community and the need of not curbing the freedom of the private practice of the physician so as to command the fullest cooperation from him for the needs and opportunities of today and tomorrow were emphasized by Doctor Roberts, who also stated that practically half the American people are not getting the care and service they need. He analyzed the hospital service of the country and the auspices under which it is administered, and said that the medical profession needs the glare of publicity, so that its problems, trials and triumphs as well as its services, may be known.

What We Spend for Health and Autos

Doctor Roberts pointed out that a medical personnel of one and one-half million persons are in medical work in this country, including 143,000 physicians, 67,334 dentists, 151,996 practical nurses and 2,600 hospital superintendents. Added to this large group he estimated another, much larger, of 1,081,000 persons, including 200,000 trained nurses, a hospital personnel of 550,000 and other assistants and technicians. The cost of medical care is nearly three billion dollars a year, he said, while the nation's income is ninety billions. He pointed out that the United States spends six

6

times as much for passenger automobiles in a year as for doctors, and remarked that this seems strangely little for health and life and cure of disease. He quoted figures showing an annual expenditure for non-government medical service of $2,130,000,000 or an average of $80 per family per year. In contrast to that he quoted figures showing non-medical expenditures of $11,700,000,000, or an average of $436 per family per year.

DOCTOR BUERKI'S ROUND TABLE

The first paper at the round table on the topic, "What Is Your Hospital Contributing to Community and Medical Education?" was given by C. J. Cummings, Tacoma General Hospital, Tacoma, Wash. Mr. Cummings discussed the hospital's obligation to its local community.

"Considered in its larger aspect, the great and primary contribution of the hospital to its community is the alleviation of suffering, the maintenance of health and the cure of disease," said Mr. Cummings. "There are, however, certain definite contributions every hospital makes to its local community: education, whereby the standards of medical and nursing practice are raised to benefit the health of not only the immediate community, but society in general; commercial enterprise, by which the hospital pays out large sums of money for supplies and for salary and wages that find their way back into the channels of trade; as a community center for service along the lines of public health and general welfare."

Paul Fesler, University of Minnesota Hospital, Minneapolis, spoke on what his hospital had been doing for the better training of internes and his paper was discussed by Dr. Harley Haynes, University of Michigan Hospital, Ann Arbor, Mich. Both men are connected with teaching hospitals and each told of the close cooperation between the medical school and the hospital in the placing and training of interns. Their problems were not the problems generally faced by the smaller institutions but much interest was manifest over the manner in which each of these Midwestern institutions fostered better intern training.

Following the discussion, Dr. Willard Rappleye, medical education committee, New Haven, Conn., spoke on the hospital's contribution to the advancement of science in medicine.

"Most hospitals," said Doctor Rappleye, "obviously cannot conduct research in all the divisions of medicine, but on the staff of most hospitals there are a few men interested in advancing our knowledge of some problem of diagnosis or treatment whose efforts should be encouraged and supported. These efforts of themselves are a vitalizing influence in the hospital program out of all proportion to the contribution which such efforts are likely to make to the science of medicine. The value of these contributions is not their number, but the accuracy with which they are made."

At Doctor Babcock's round table on Tuesday, group nursing as a means toward the reduction of the cost of illness was discussed by L. C. Vonder Heidt, West Suburban Hospital, Oak Park, Ill., and E. Muriel Anscombe, Jewish Hospital, St. Louis.

Mr. Vonder Heidt described the plan of group nursing in effect at his hospital and pointed out that it had met with success, the average for a four-year period showing a small surplus and this with approximately a 55 per cent average annual occupancy. Group nursing is carried on in one eighteen-room unit of the hospital, with twelve graduate nurses and one supervisor. The nurses receive $125 a month, with board and laundry, rooming out at their own expense. The working schedule calls for eight hours of service a day, eight nurses doing day duty, two night duty and two relief.

Group nursing must be definitely confined to some particular section of the institution and cannot be practiced promiscuously throughout the various patient floors, Mr. Vonder Heidt said.

Miss Anscombe stated that in her opinion group nursing is both feasible and practical and is probably the best method of supplying good and inexpensive care for the patient of moderate means. She believes also that it may help control the supply of student nurses and may permit more selectivity among them. Graduates, she feels, should welcome the system as it reduces their working day by four hours. Another of its advantages is that it gives the nurse an opportunity to study disease more intensively, for with group nursing the nurse has many different types of cases to study. Miss Anscombe discussed the different methods of establishing the system in different institutions and stressed the importance of having proper utility rooms and proper working units. Group nursing is here to stay and to reduce costs, she believes.

Doctor Babcock told how the group nursing system is carried out at this institution, where the service has been in existence for three years and the nurses are on eight-hour duty. John Smith, Hahnemann Hospital, Philadelphia, James R. Mays, New York City, and Jessie J. Turnbull, Elizabeth Steel Magee Hospital, Pittsburgh, contributed to the discussion of this subject.

8

Why maintaining a high quality of service is essential to a successful hospital was the theme of the paper given by F. O. Bates, Roper Hospital, Charleston, S. C. .

The secret of the high quality of service that is essential to a successful hospital is the coordination of all departments from the administrative office to the obscure carpenter shop, he emphasized. They must all work in complete harmony for the good of the patient. "We must not forget the human element," he said. "We should let it sway us always. We must as vigilantly supervise the patient's case as many seem to supervise the patient's bills. Our enthusiastic striving for scientific improvement and experimentation must be guided by a sympathetic consideration of our patients. The hospital, the practitioner and even the medical society, are interdependent units; when they function in unison as a harmonious whole, many of our difficulties will be solved, our institutions will be better served and the patient will reap the highest type of service."

Dr. Babcock was coordinator at a round table on "Problems of the Patient of Moderate Means."

The discussion was opened by a paper by Dr. S. S. Goldwater, consultant, New York City, read in the absence of the author by Dr. J. B. Howland, Peter Bent Brigham Hospital, Boston. Doctor Goldwater analyzed the effort that hospitals have made so far to deal with the problem of providing adequate care at a cost in keeping with modest incomes.

As a relief measure he suggested a system of insurance or mutual aid. Insurance against sickness and especially against hospital costs would introduce in the budget of the family of modest means an item that could be borne without great hardship. It is amazing, he said, that so little has been done in this direction in a country where voluntary life insurance is almost universally practiced and where accident insurance has been popularly accepted for years.

Doctor Goldwater's paper on this subject will appear in full in an early issue of The Modern Hospital.

Robert Jolly, Baptist Hospital, Houston, Tex., followed Doctor Goldwater. He crticized persons of moderate means who paid little attention to their annual budget, making few, if any, provisions for illness costs. To educate these persons, the hospital has an educational job ahead of it, he said.

The discussion was taken up at this point by J. B. Franklin.

The entire solution of the problem of providing care for patients of moderate means is not an obligation of the hospital, Mr. Franklin emphasized. The individual himself can help by making provision for sickness in his monthly expense budget and by choosing accommodations within his income. Philanthropists can help by special gifts to maintain beds and by general endowments to hospitals; doctors can help by cooperating with hospitals in limiting their fees and hospitals can help by providing accommodations and service at graduated prices to suit the pocketbook of the patient. This service can be furnished in ward beds, semi-private beds and in small private rooms, all at a cost considerably below the usual hospital charges.

Probably the wisest plan, said Mr. Franklin, is to provide a separate building for this type of patient. Only a few hospitals, however, can afford a separate building. But many hospitals can designate certain wards, semi-private and private rooms for such service and fix the prices according to the cost of maintaining such accommodations, or at rates below the usual charges.

Advantages of social service to the hospital was the next topic considered at this round table. Dr. J. Moss Beeler, Spartanburg General Hospital, Spartanburg, S. C., was the first speaker. He described in detail the physical plant and organization of the institution of which he is superintendent and indicated what should be the relation of the social worker to the hospital, to the physician and to the public. He pointed out the responsibility of the social worker in helping the patient to adjust himself to his situation in the hospital and in helping the family to get the right mental attitude in facing the circumstances surrounding sickness. It is a part of the social worker's duty to classify patients so that the hospital may be enabled to grade its charges appropriately, he said. He also pointed out that the social service worker keeps down the cost of the hospital by keeping out many charity patients through preventive work and noticing symptoms early in the development of a disease. She is a link between the hospital and the community. Doctor Beeler's paper was discussed by Doctor Rankin.

ENDOWED NURSES

The following letter from Mr. Bacon and resultant editorial appearing in the Chicago Tribune of August 11, 1930, have already brought forth promises of two more endowed nurses.

THE NURSE IN RESERVE

Chicago, Aug. 7.—Chicago has 136 hospitals, caring for some 300,000 patients annually, spending about $27,000,000 every year for their maintenance, and with approximately $80,000,000 invested in lands, buildings and equipment. Fifty-five of these institutions are organized as charitable corporations, either independently or under the auspices of churches, offering a total of 9,049 beds, or slightly more than 40 per cent of the total bed capacity of the city. (Report by Margaret Lovell Plumley and Michael M. Davis to the Institute of Medicine of Chicago.) These include some of the finest plants in `the world, impressive monuments to medical progress and private philanthropy.

In the charitable hospitals Chicago physicians and surgeons have given and are giving their services according to the ancient laws of medicine. But what of the nurse? Her rate of compensation is fixed, affording no more than a living wage. She cannot give of her time and skill without regular payment and survive. Yet in some cases her services are indispensable, not as a floor nurse but in the capacity of a private or special nurse giving full attention to a patient during a few days or a few hours of critical condition.

Some thirteen years ago a Chicagoan hit upon the answer to this problem and inaugurated the first philanthropy of its kind when she endowed a nurse for work in the wards of the Presbyterian Hospital. By setting up a sum of $35,000 Miss Helen North provided sufficient income to pay the salary of one nurse for front line duty the year round. Wherever death is nearest this nurse goes. She is the reserve force which the hospital superintendent throws into the balance when a man, woman, or child goes deep into the shadow and the forces of dissolution are dangerously near a victory.

A day, perhaps two, and the crisis is past. The Helen North nurse, as she is called, does not always win. In the vast majority of cases, however, the patient in the modern hospital survives. The next day finds the nurse fighting the same battle at another bedside. She cares for approximately 250 patients in the course of a year. Time and again the attending physician says, "Mark up another score. That thyroidectomy would never have pulled through without you."

11

Another front line nurse was provided in 1921 by an endowment undertaken by Presbyterian nurses with the aid of the woman's board of the hospital. She is known as the Gladys Foster nurse, in memory of a member of the nursing school who fell in line of duty during the influenza epidemic of 1918. In March, 1930, another was added by endowment of Mrs. Hamill, being known as the Ernest A. Hamill nurse.

So far as is known, these three in Chicago are the only examples of the endowed hospital nurse. Yet it would seem highly desirable that this should become a common form of philanthropic expression. Under the pressure of providing the utmost in modern hospital equipment, the art of nursing, one of the fundamental requirements of the very sick patient, should not be overlooked. And while the welfare of the patient is the first consideration, the practice of endowed nurses will also provide some definite increase of nursing education due to the fact that only the well qualified nurse will secure the endowed position.

Asa S. Bacon, Superintendent Presbyterian Hospital.

EDITORIAL

The Emergency Nurse

A communication from Superintendent Bacon of the Presbyterian Hospital published in the Voice of the People today contains some interesting facts and suggests a new form of practical philanthropy, the endowment of what we may describe in military analogy as a nursing reserve. There are many patients both in and out of hospitals who cannot afford a private nurse, but whose condition has reached a crisis during which special nursing may mean the difference between life and death. Here is when the hospital, which has nurses endowed for such service and therefore not engaged with either the routine duties of the hospital service or with private cases, can, as it were, move its troops to the point of emergency.

Mr. Bacon says a fund for such service was provided 13 years ago by Miss Helen North, and we agree with him that it opens up a most promising field of service which ought to be greatly extended. People of means who wish to assist in the war against human suffering and extend skilled aid to the sick of small means should consider this plan.

REDUCING ILLNESS COSTS BY MEANS OF ORGANIZED NURSING SERVICE

By Daisy Dean Urch, R.N., A.M.

Visiting Instructor, Department of Nursing Education, University of Washington College of Sciences, Seattle

To paraphrase the famous message of Dr. Olin West, secretary, American Medical Association, "The one great outstanding problem facing the nursing profession today is that involved in the giving of skilled nursing care to all of the people, rich and poor, at a cost which can be reasonably met by them in their respective stations of life." How this can be done and how at the same time nurses can receive adequate incomes has been the topic for countless discussions and much experimentation during the last decade.

All nurses are familiar with the Committee on the Grading of Nursing Schools which is in the fourth year of its five-year program of a nationwide study of nursing. Their reports on supply and demand of nurses, the economic status of the nurse and nursing education conditions are worthy of careful study. Fortunately for all concerned, the committee is supported by physicians and lay persons as well as by nurses. We may therefore expect from it exact data and unprejudiced opinions, and we are, I believe, getting just what we expect. Also in the experiments which have been undertaken to cut down nursing costs, the cooperation of physicians, patients, nurses and hospital executives has been secured. This all augers well for the solution of this problem. It is important, I believe, that we rid ourselves of emotional bias and look the facts squarely in the face.

In order that we may better understand the ineffectual wailing over the "commercializing" and "overeducation" of the nurse at the expense of the patient, let us find out the reason for it. One of the reasons is, I believe, the fact that the nursing profession has its roots in the church with its ideals of service—service without pay other than spiritual rewards. Since the time of Phoebe, the first Christian visiting nurse, to the present time, we have had those who nursed for little or nothing. Free hospital care has been given by religious groups, and kindly neighbors have contributed their services in homes. Our endowed or tax supported hospitals and visiting nurse associations have carried on the good work. Physicians have given their services, and thus for centuries the great majority of patients have not had the painful experience of parting with their money to pay for care when they were ill. Two other factors influ-

13

ence this attitude. No one enjoys illness, and most people believe that disease just comes and that they are in no wise to blame for it. Hence, a general attitude of evading this responsibility has developed.

In 1929, as much money was spent for cigars and cigarettes as for hospital bills, twice as much for movie tickets and four times as much for gasoline and automobiles. A man goes to a hotel and cheerfully pays $7 to $10 a day for a room and meals with no personal service. The same man will go to a hospital and for an equal amount of money will expect as good a room, as expensive meals served in bed, and the personal services of a nurse, dietitian, technician and all the expensive hospital equipment thrown in.

The problem has developed from an attitude toward paying for illness that is unwholesome and unfair. I think the solution is publicity to bring about a frank facing of facts with the hope of changing this attitude and bringing about a sense of fair play on the part of patients and their relatives and friends. Physicians and nurses receive expensive educations, which represent long hard work, application to duty and self-denial, as well as money. They are expected to pay their personal bills. Recent studies have shown that the average private duty nurse works twenty-one days a month. She must pay for room and food for thirty days a month. While the patient is paying $7.50 a day the nurse receives only $6 of the fee. That gives her a yearly income of about $1,300, without vacation or days off with pay. The average yearly income of physicians in proportion to the expense of their education is about the same.

Furthermore, much of the sickness, the expense of which physicians and nurses are expected to bear, is preventable. Immunization against at least four of the communicable diseases is posible, and a dozen others can be prevented by clean sane living. Abstinence from intoxicating drinks and other dissipations and careful driving can still further lower the amount of sickness. The twenty-four dollars per annum paid by the average person for sickness could probably be reduced at least one-half if these precautions were universally taken. If the average person would invest one-half the money he spends for cigarettes, radios, automobiles or movie tickets in a good insurance policy he would unquestionably be able to pay for his illness.

A fairly large proportion of the cost of illness (an estimated 30 per cent) is the hospital bill. This could be lessened if hospitals were more efficiently managed. Practically all hospital executives learn their jobs by the trial and error method and at the expense of the institution they serve. There is also much waste of time and

14

energy and strain on dispositions because of poor construction and inconvenient arrangement in hospital buildings. Why anyone should think that a doctor, a nurse, a business man, a broken-down minister or a vote-getter should by virtue of being any one of these things necessarily be a good hospital executive is beyond comprehension. To be a skillful doctor or an expert nurse does not imply that a man or a woman has executive ability. Yet both doctors and nurses with executive ability make splendid hospital administrators after they have learned the art. It is poor economics, however, for an institution to allow them to learn it at the institution's expense. We have schools for preparing physicians, nurses, teachers, engineers, even business men. Why not schools for training hospital executives? In the planning of hospital buildings, all the workers who know the details of their departments and who work there should be called in conference with the architects. No one person could possibly be expert in matters relating to every department.

Then there is the economic waste in nursing service. With the present accounting systems in hospitals, it is not possible to tell the exact cost of nursing service. Except in the case of special nurses, the cost of nursing is grouped with the charge for room, food, food service and upkeep of hospitals. Even the special's board bill is a much mooted question. We know, however, that the nurse cannot charge less than she is now charging.

FLEXIBLE NURSING SERVICE NEEDED

It is also true that while the nurse is working longer hours and receiving smaller pay than any other worker, much of this time is of no value to the patient. The patient's husband may be paying for twenty-four hours of nursing service a day while she actually needs only four hours. But nursing in hourly packages is provided in few hospitals or homes, and patients are inclined to want frills and de luxe care and the prestige of a special nurse. It is pleasing to have these little personal attetions, "to be wrapped in the cotton wool of nursing service," as Doctor Burgess expresses it. Then there is the real fear that comes to the patient and his family and drives them to make any sacrifice in order to have a nurse at hand every moment of the patient's illness.

The answer to this problem is a nursing service for both the hospital and the home that is flexible enough to meet the actual needs of all the patients in the amounts and at the times and places required. This, of course, calls for engineering on a large and far-sighted basis and the concerted efforts of the best minds in the

15

community. Real statesmanship is needed. I should like to see established a glorified bureau of nursing service, with a board of trustees, including physicians, surgeons, public health officials, hospital executives, business men, public-spirited citizens and nurses (including those engaged in institutional, public and private duty work).

This bureau would serve a large area, would have a revolving fund and would plan its budget to provide for nursing by the hour or the job in homes and hospitals and for public health agencies. The hourly, visiting and special nurses would receive regular salaries paid by the bureau. Public health organizations and hospitals would pay their regular staff as at present and would call on the bureau for extra help when such was needed. Individual patients in both homes and hospitals could buy nursing service from the bureau by the hour, whether it were for one hour or for twenty-four hours. Each bureau could survey its community and keep an adequate number of the needed types of nurses. Vacations could be given at quiet periods. The personal touch need not be lost. Does this sound too millennial?

As a matter of fact every phase of this plan is now being successfully carried out, except the central board with the funds. We have visiting nursing and hourly nursing and group nursing and general duty nursing now. The University Hospital, Ann Arbor, Mich., the Henry Ford Hospital, Detroit, and many others have salaried special nurses. The New York, Chicago and San Francisco Visiting Nurses' Associations and many registries provide nursing in the homes. These arrangements have been worked out in response to demands and have succeeded because they met the actual needs of the people. There are now larger needs and we must meet them. If the whole community were organized some of the most difficult problems would be solved.

PROBLEM IS MANYSIDED

I see five phases of the problem confronting us. The solution is a challenge that can be met only by good team work on the part of all groups concerned—social workers, physicians, hospital executives, nurses and patients (including prospective patients).

First, patients do not like to pay for their illnesses and too frequently try to evade their responsibility for doing so. Yet they willingly pay for cigarettes, cosmetics, radios, automobiles, gasoline, chewing gum and movies. The public should be educated to recognize the value of good medical, nursing and hospital care and to be as willing to pay for it as for other luxuries.

16

Second, illness with its inevitable cost could be greatly lessened if people lived hygienically and availed themselves of preventive measures now known to medical science. There should be more intensive programs in schools and elsewhere to induce people to prevent disease and accident and to value health.

Third, provision for paying for illness is usually not made. Illness is made an excuse for an orgy of needless expenditure. About one-fifth of the cost is spent on nostrums and quacks. People must learn to budget or insure for illness and to make plans for spending this money wisely and well. They must also learn to pay for all they demand.

Fourth, hospitals and hospital equipment are expensive. Because of poor planning and amateur management, most hospitals are needlessly costly. Physicians and nurses with ability and taste along this line should take special courses to prepare themselves to become hospital executives. Nurses, dietitians and other hospital experts should assist in planning, building, equipping and supplying hospitals.

Fifth, nursing is expert trained personal service. Although it is estimated that only 7 per cent of the total cost of illness is paid to both trained and practical nurses, this is unevenly distributed and falls heavily at inopportune times. There should be organized community projects whereby hourly or visiting nursing in homes and group or hourly nursing in hospitals can be obtained on an adequate, reasonable, not de luxe, basis.

—Courtesy of the Nursing and the Hospital Section of The Modern Hospital, conducted by M. Helena McMillan, R.N., Director, School of Nursing, Presbyterian Hospital, Chicago.

HOURLY NURSING SERVICE OF CHICAGO AIDED BY ROSENWALD

The Hourly Nursing Service of Chicago, sponsored by the Joint Committee on Hourly Nursing, has received from the Julius Rosenwald Foundation financial assistance that will cover all of the promotional expenses and half of the operating expenses of this organization.

Miriam Ames will assume the position as executive director on January 1, 1931.

The Hourly Nursing Service was initiated by the joint committee representing the Central Council for Nursing Education and the first district of the Illinois State Nurses' Association, in order to bring the best nursing service within the reach of persons of

17

modest means and also to furnish nursing by appointment where full-time nursing is not needed.

Nursing groups throughout the country will watch with keen interest the development of this project because of its twofold purpose. The interest of the Rosenwald Foundation was secured because the service attempts to meet the nursing needs of the family of modest means.

SOCIAL SERVICE

Miss Isabel Bering comes to us from the Billings Memorial Hospital, University of Chicago, to take charge of the Social Service Department. The Woman's Board takes pleasure in welcoming Miss Bering and in pledging their support and cooperation in her work.

BOOKS WANTED FOR THE LIBRARY

The library will appreciate donations of good books on any of the following subjects. A few examples of titles are listed, but other standard works are just as acceptable.

HISTORY AND POLITICS
   Davis—History of France
   Bassett—Short History of the United States
   Bryce—American Commonwealth
   Breasted—Ancient Times
   Beard—American Government and Politics
   Hazen—Europe Since 1815

BIOGRAPHY

TRAVEL

ESSAYS

PHILOSOPHY

POETRY, especially collections by various authors

PLAYS, especially collections

ARTS—Painting, sculpturing, music, household decoration, etc.

SCIENCE—Astronomy, geology, nature, etc.

STANDARD FICTION, not only American, but also English, Russian, French and Scandinavian translations.

Books Must Be in Good Condition

THE AMERICAN NURSES' ASSOCIATION

Children's Hospital,
18th and Bainbridge Streets,
Philadelphia, Penn.

Miss M. Helena McMillan, ·   July 7th, 1930.
Presbyterian Hospital,
Chicago, Ill.

My dear Miss McMillan:

At a meeting of the Board of Directors of the American Nurses' Association held in Milwaukee, Wisconsin, June 14, 1930, the following resolution was adopted:

> That a letter of congratulation be sent to Miss Helena McMillan, the Director of the School of Nursing in the Presbyterian Hospital of Chicago, upon the type of women whom she has sent out into the nursing profession and upon their achievements and upon the fine records which they are continuing to make.

The women whom the Board had particularly in mind at this time were the following: Miss Elnora E. Thompson, R.N., Miss Mabel M. Dunlop, R.N., Mrs. Alma H. Scott, R.N., Mrs. Helen W Munson, R.N.

May I add my personal note of appreciation at this time?

Yours sincerely,

SUSAN C. FRANCIS, R.N.,
Secretary.

19

NURSES IN FOREIGN FIELDS

Class of 1912—Mrs. Margaret Corrette Owen — 17 years, Assuit, Egypt

Class of 1914—Miss M. Edna Burgess—15 years, Tabriz, Persia

Class of 1916—Miss Verda F. Hickox—1½ years, Siriraj Hospital, Bangkok, Siam

Class of 1918—Miss Gertrude E. Kellogg—11 years, Fenchow, China

Class of 1919—Miss Ida Marie Seymour—11 years, Tsining, China

Class of 1920—Miss Elsie Moser—3 years, Haiti; 1 year, Greece

Class of 1921—Miss Mary E. Bricker—5 years, India

Class of 1922—Miss Leila Clark—8 years, Lahore, India

Class of 1922—Miss Gwynaeth Porter — 8 years, Taxilla, Punjab, India

Class of 1923—Miss Isla F. Knight—2 years, Sanjan, Thana District, India

Class of 1923—Miss Glyde Leach—to Peiping Union Hospital, China, September, 1930

Class of 1924—Mrs. Ruth Hinegardner—to Peiping Union Hospital, China, September, 1930

Class of 1925—Miss Mildred B. Porter—2 years, Siriraj Hospital, Bangkok, Siam

Class of 1927—Mrs. Helen McCuish Oltman—Amoy, China, 1930

Class of 1928—Miss Mary Lillian Young — 2 years, Natal, South Africa

Class of 1928—Miss Winona Hayenga—1 year, Ebolowa, Cameroun, West Africa

FREE BEDS AND MEMBERS

A donation of $50,000 entitles the donor to name a twelve-bed ward, which shall remain as a perpetual memorial to the donor, or any other individual he wishes.

A donation of $20,000 carries the same privileges for a four or six-bed ward.

A donation of $10,000 entitles the donor to designate a room in the Private Pavilion which shall be named as desired by the donor and remain as a perpetual memorial.

A donation of $7,500 designates a bed in perpetuity.

A donation of $5,000 designates a bed during one life.

A donation of $5,000 designates a bed in the Children's Ward in perpetuity.

A donation of $300 annually designates a free bed in the general wards.

A donation of $100 or more constitutes the donor a life member of the institution.

A yearly donation of $10 constitutes an annual member.

FORM OF BEQUEST

I give and bequeath to the Presbyterian Hospital of the City of Chicago, incorporated under the law of the State of Illinois, the sum of ⁚.. Dollars, to be applied to the use and benefit of the said hospital, under the direction of the managers thereof.

FORM OF DEVISE

I give and devise to the Presbyterian Hospital of the City of Chicago, incorporated under the law of the State of Illinois, all that, etc. [*describe the property*], to be had and holden to the said the Presbyterian Hospital of the City of Chicago, and their successors and assigns, for the use and benefit of the said hospital.

21

ALUMNÆ NOTES

The annual Home Coming of the School of Nursing will be held at the Sprague Home, November 11, 1930.

There will be "Open" House after ten o'clock in the morning. A special "home talent" program of music and readings is being arranged for the evening entertainment.

* * *

The Alumnæ realized the sum of $136.85 from the Rummage Sale which was held at the Central Free Dispensary, October 28 and 29.

We wish to thank everyone who sent contributions and also those who assisted at the sale.

* * *

The first Monday in December the usual sale of cold cream and candy made by the student nurses will be held in the corridor of the fifth floor of the hospital.

Food will also be sold on the first floor, under the direction of Miss Aylward.

1908

Mrs. C. S. Griffith (Gertrude E. Craig), Knoxville, Tennessee, finds time in addition to her home duties to fill a position of supervision with the Public Health Nursing Service there, and is planning on further work and a new position.

1911

Ida E. Twedten is now located in southern Virginia in a mountain mission school at Konnarock, serving as a community nurse. During the summer while school was closed, they conducted nine Daily Vacation Bible Schools in isolated mountain communities. Nursing classes for the mothers were conducted by Miss Twedten, some of these mothers walking three miles over rough mountain roads in order to attend the classes. There is no doctor at Konnorock and all minor injuries are brought to the little dispensary. A Mothers' Club has also been organized and interesting plans for the coming year are being made.

1912

Mrs. C. A. Owen (Margaret J. Corette) has returned from Egypt and is at her home at 618 South Second Avenue, Washington, Iowa.

1913

Mrs. C. W. Hyer (E. Burdena Johnston, 1913) writes from Douglas, Arizona, that she has been in public school work there for the past eight years. She has not been in Chicago for ten years but through her classmates does keep in touch with the activities of the school.

1915

Mrs. J. M. Liddell (Mabel G. Browne), San Diego, California, interested at all times in nursing activities, is registering in the state of California. She mentions seeing Miss Julia S. Chubbuck (1908), who is quite well and happy.

1916

Mrs. E. Gruetzman (Mary Rust) has accepted the position of Supervisor of Nurses at the County Santa Clara Sanatorium, California.

From Mary Bissett come some interesting letters. Her new work is at the Stillman Institute, Tuscaloosa, Alabama, in charge of a small hospital and training school for nurses which was opened September 1, in connection with church home mission work in behalf of the Negro.

A nice new building awaited Miss Bissett, but no equipment and it may mean some little time before it may be opened for service.

Her time is well filled, however, having been appointed Red Cross nurse by special enrollment, whereby she may teach Home Hygiene and Care of the Sick under national supervision. Two classes have already been started, one in Senior High School and the other at Junior College.

She also has a small group of student nurses for whom she has found ways and means of starting on their nursing career with the help of material at hand.

She believes the work will grow and that the opportunity for an out-clinic and social service department will open up.

We certainly wish Miss Bissett all the success possible in this new field.

1918

Miss Gertrude E. Kellogg has been in the United States this summer and called on us several times and did some observing in the various departments of the hospital.

By this time, no doubt, she is again at her work in Fenchow, Shansi, China.

1919

M. Elizabeth Nicholas, New Haven, Connecticut, has been doing private duty, but plans on going to New York City and working there.

1920

From Ann Trudgian Bates we hear that she has been with the city schools of Tucson, Arizona, last year and will continue this work this year also. She seems much in love with her work as also with the desert and desert life. She states that the two hospitals in Tucson, besides the government hospital, have improved a great deal the last few years and that work for the private duty nurse is not very promising this year.

1921

Hazel Taylor has returned to Shanghai, China, after a year's furlough in this country, resuming her work as supervisor of the public health department of the Margaret Williams Hospital.

1923

Gladys Baldwin, for a number of years on the operating room staff of the Presbyterian Hospital, Chicago, on September 1, 1930, began her work as supervisor of the operating rooms at the Billings Memorial Hospital, University of Chicago.

Catharine A. Clow is at the State Normal School, Fredonia, New York, as nurse in the Health Department and also is teaching biology.

Glye Leach has resigned her position in the operating rooms at the Billings Memorial Hospital and has accepted a similar position at the Peiping Union Medical College, Peiping, China.

1924

Alethea Boggess has left her work in the Elizabeth General Hospital, New Jersey, and is now assistant supervisor of the Pediatric Department at the Bellevue Hospital, New York City, carrying also one subject at Teacher's College, Columbia, with the aim, in time, of securing her degree.

1925

Ruth Jackson, having completed the course in the giving of anaesthetics, St. Joseph's Hospital, Chicago, has accepted a position as an anaesthetist at Michael Reese Hospital, Chicago.

Ada Quinnell, head nurse at the Central Free Dispensary, was granted the opportunity of attending a four weeks' course at the Vanderbilt Clinic, New York City, this summer, observing the work in the various clinics. She was one of the first two nurses to take this work at the Vanderbilt Clinics.

Mildred B. Porter, Siriraj Hospital, Bangkok, Siam, keeps us informed of their latest activities. A recent letter reads as follows: "We are finding the work here extremely interesting. The Siamese girls are certainly becoming more interested in professional trainings.

"We are planning to build a new nurses' residence very soon. We are waiting for the end of the rainy season and the start of the dry season. Our new residence will accommodate 125 student nurses, 30 general duty nurses, 32 staff nurses, and have private apartments for the superintendent and the matron. We are planning it entirely for the Siamese. We have a very nice site overlooking the river. It is very near the hospital.

"A generous friend has donated a plot of land at Bo Fai, at the seaside. We are now raising money to build a bungalow for a vacation and convalescent home for our nurses. We need this very much as so many of the girls come from poor homes."

1926

Mary Spires has been appointed superintendent of the Eye, Ear, Nose and Throat Hospital of Houston, Texas.

R. Luella Brohaugh, from Portland, Oregon, is considering taking the course in Public Health Nursing, either at Portland or at the University of Washington.

1928

Maurine Hickman is situated with the McCormick Harvester Company as an industrial nurse.

Ruth Burr has received an appointment at the Government Hospital at Dulce, New Mexico. At first her work was that of substituting at the Tuberculosis Sanitarium for Apache Indian Children and later a permanent position at the hospital. She too writes enthusiastically of the country and the outdoor sports.

Cornelia Mokma, a classmate, is also in Dulce.

Gladys M. Kartzke has a position on the Public Health Staff at Cleveland, Ohio, for the coming year. Last year she was a supervisor at the Glenville Hospital, Cleveland, assisting with the medical lectures and teaching medical nursing.

1929

Anna A. Heilig is night supervisor at the St. Joseph's Sanitarium, St. Joseph, Michigan.

Alice Richards and Louise Anderson are doing nursing work in Honolulu at the Kapiolani Maternity Hospital.

1930

Mary Hamilton has a position on the staff of Smith College.

Ruth Moon is spending the winter in Tucson, Arizona.

MARRIAGES

Bess Everett (1920) married to Mr. Donald G. Wilmarth, August 9, 1930, at De Kalb, Illinois.

Elizabeth D. Risser (1929) married to Dr. Clayton J. Lundy, September 27, 1930, at Chareton, Iowa.

Arline J. Deck (1927) married to Mr. Jaro J. Cermak, July 12, 1930, at Berwyn, Illinois.

Genevieve M. Crockett (1925) married to Dr. Lloyd Kenney, August 13, 1930, at Beloit, Wisconsin.

Lyla Hovey (1928) married to Dr. Otto N. Glesne, August 22, 1930.

Viola J. Replogle (1926) married to Mr. P. Roy Westerlund, October 16, 1930, at Red Oak, Iowa.

Muriel M. Perry (1929) married to Mr. Harold Barbee Mitchell, June 14, 1930, Benton Harbor, Michigan.

Harriet E. Hunt (1927) married to Mr. Russell C. Smith, June 7, 1930, De Kalb, Illinois.

Lavina I. Beck (1920) married to Mr. Royal W. Davenport, August 16, 1930, New York City.

Geda Myhre (1922) married to Mr. Burnett E. Green, June 3, 1930, at the University of Chicago Chapel, Chicago.

Erma LeBert (1928) married to Mr. Wm. T. Brannon, July 5, 1930, at Chicago.

Florence E. West (1924) married to Mr. Paul Sonneman, September 6, 1930, at Los Angeles, California.

Juanita Austin (1928) married to Kenneth F. Sanders, September 30, 1930.

Alice Dolan (1930) married to Mr. Raymond McCormick, May, 1930.

DEATHS

Erna McDonald (1922) died at her home, 1529 N. Union Street, Decatur, Illinois, June 27, 1930.

Josephine A. Toms (1912) died at her home Richland Center, Wisconsin, September, 1930.

BIRTHS

Mr. and Mrs. W. R. Sproul (Frances Carlson, 1925), a son, Robert Francis, June 23, 1930.

Dr. and Mrs. Lorne W. Mason (Alice Hamilton, 1929), a son, James Hamilton, June 5, 1930.

Mr. and Mrs. H. M. Franz (Ruth Braun, 1921), a son, David Wagner, October 11, 1930.

Mr. and Mrs. M. D. Bone (Cleland B. Winans, 1927), a daughter, Carolynn Gratia, August 7, 1930.

Dr. and Mrs. E. S. Olson (Lillian Olson, 1924), a son, Ernest S., Jr., August 2, 1930.

Lightning Source UK Ltd.
Milton Keynes UK
UKHW020024181218
334174UK00013B/2044/P